Schools That Do Too Much

Schools That Do Too Much

Wasting Time and Money
in Schools and What We
Can All Do about It

Etta Kralovec

Beacon Press BOSTON

Beacon Press
25 Beacon Street
Boston, Massachusetts 02108-2892
www.beacon.org

Beacon Press books
are published under the auspices of
the Unitarian Universalist Association of Congregations.

06 05 04 03   8 7 6 5 4 3 2 1

This book is printed on acid-free paper that meets the uncoated
paper ANSI/NISO specifications for permanence as revised in 1992.

Composition by Wilsted & Taylor Publishing Services

LIBRARY OF CONGRESS CATALOGING-IN-PUBLICATION DATA
Kralovec, Etta.
      Schools that do too much : wasting time and money in schools,
and what we can all do about it / Etta Kralovec.
          p. cm.
Includes bibliographical references.
      ISBN 0-8070-3150-x (hard : alk. paper)
      1. Schedules, School—United States. 2. Time management—United States.
3. Schools—United States—Finance. 4. Education—United States—Costs.
5. School management and organization—United States. I. Title.

To Maxine Greene,
who has guided my sense of the possible
and my refusal of the given

Contents

Introduction

I spent more than a year of my life talking to thousands of people about homework. I had just published *The End of Homework,* in which my coauthor and I argued that homework disrupts families, overburdens children, and limits learning. I was gratified and amazed by the energy of the discussions the book generated among parents, teachers, and school people of all kinds. There was, for the most part, easy agreement that homework loads were far too heavy, even as there was debate about what to do about it.

But almost always something happened in these discussions: the topic shifted at some point from how students spend time after school to how they spend—and should spend—their time in school. At PTO meetings, teacher in-service sessions, Rotary Clubs, and book talks in local bookstores, I listened as parents and teachers in communities as diverse as the South Side of Chicago; Newton, Massachusetts; Camden, Maine; and Laguna Beach, California, talked about their struggles to make their children's education meaningful and substantial in the face of large class size, truncated school days, and misspent school dollars. I heard the lament over misplaced school priorities and a high school culture that glorifies sports heroes. I heard parents give testimony—with relief in their voices—to the value and benefit of home-schooling their children. Over and over again I heard the same stories on talk radio shows—in the United Kingdom, on CBC radio in Canada, and in the United States—as parents and teachers struggled to make sense of what happens in the eight hours our children are in school.

Parents and school people alike saw that behind the debates about homework lay bigger issues of what our priorities are for schools. They demonstrated the need for new ways of talking not only about time but about money, and about how we spend these precious resources.

This book is designed to start that national conversation. I argue that American schools have evolved ways of spending time and money that systematically undermine learning. By trying to do too much, they end up doing too little of what matters. I don't argue for spending more time in school and more money spent on schools. I argue for radically rethinking the way we use the time and money we have.

Schools That Do Too Much is like a microscope trained on the daily life of schools at the cellular level, uncovering the routines and structural apparatus that have become commonplace and that operate virtually unnoticed. These structures and activities, sometimes called the rituals of schooling, constrain innovation and limit learning. By consuming a large portion of the school day these ritualized ways of "doing" school compete with the real work at hand—teaching and learning.

The ways we spend time and money in schools are not facts of nature. They are decisions we have made as communities, and they are decisions we can unmake. We need to see what's wrong with the way we spend time and money and we need to give teachers, parents, and community members a new set of questions to ask, because we all have a part to play in the solutions. This book looks at a wide range of educational research findings about the nature of the school day and its impact on students and their academic achievement. The strong, even radical, recommendations I argue for are premised on the notion that real change takes *real* change. Not for the fainthearted, the recommendations ask the entire community to shoulder a greater share of the responsibility for student learning. *Schools That Do Too Much* is designed to give those interested in improving schools in their communities the tools they need to improve educational opportunities for students by unburdening the school.

"Time is money" is a saying most of us have grown up with. When it comes to schooling, "Money is time" is equally accurate. Where we put our education dollars determines how students spend their time in school. Yet often we think too haphazardly and unsystematically about these two fundamental aspects of schooling and how they shape our students' educational opportunities.

In our personal lives, we discuss time and money issues in fairly hard-nosed terms: costs and benefits, opportunity costs, tradeoffs. If we go on a vacation this year, we can't get a new computer. If we renew a subscription to a magazine that we have been getting for twelve years, we know we can't order that new magazine we've been wanting to read. Companies make financial decisions after carefully weighing the costs and the risks against the potential gains.

But when it comes to schooling issues, public dialogue steers clear of hard-nosed budget and scheduling discussion, focusing instead on political and programmatic conundrums. When school budgets are discussed in public meetings, we often see the worst in a community as older citizens are pitted against parents and class divisions splinter the community. Union negotiations, state and federal mandates, and local practice all shape the way school budgets ultimately look as they are presented to voters, but these efforts lack coordination. Board members who work with school administrators on budgeting have a political constituency to answer to and local property taxes to think about. Spending decisions, shaped by our beliefs about what schools are supposed to do, determine the structure of the school day, the nature of the academic program, and the very culture of school life. In truth, however, we disagree radically about what the mission of schools is and in the end our schools carry mixed messages. The result is a kind of chaos, a set of insufficiently thought through compromises.

We sense something is wrong in the ways schools are typically organized—and I hope to show just how true this is—but typically we only tinker at the margins: Often we heap new programs onto old, shaving off a few minutes of each class period and shifting the responsibility for the leftover work to parents in the form of homework assignments. If we need to cut the school budget, we cut a few dollars from each program, or rob Peter to pay Paul this year and then rob Paul to pay Peter next. The deplorable state of our aging school buildings stretches school budgets beyond taxpayers' ability and willingness to pay for improvements. Rarely do we conduct a systematic analysis of the way teachers and students spend the school day or the way we allocate school dollars. Children's birthday parties, fundraising for worthy causes, character education, and drug education all compete with core academic learning for the hours in the school day. In terms of school dollars, this is not to say that we don't scrutinize school finances; we do, and to a ridiculous extreme. At one school board meeting I attended recently in a community with an $8 million school budget, the audience engaged in a twenty-minute heated debate about a fifty-six-dollar expenditure in the library budget for a particular periodical. This kind of community discussion is what passes for a budgeting process in many of our schools. Unfortunately, it actually precludes hard questions about how our school dollars and days should be spent. Tightly controlled by administrators, community budgeting discussions continue year after year down the well-worn path of slicing a few thousand dollars off a multimillion-dollar budget. This gives the appearance of fiscal responsibility and conservation of public dollars; in reality such an incremental budgeting process effectively strangles school innovation and change.

The chaotic life in schools today is our inheritance from a century of this continual tinkering with public schools and public dissatisfaction with the result. Add something this year, add something else next year, keep programs in place because of "tradition," and you have, I will argue, the overburdened school, the school that tries to do too much—and ironically ends up not getting many of the results we care most about.

Maybe we don't have systematic school budget discussions because we know that in order to have this discussion we must examine some of our educational traditions and most cherished educational practices. Questioning these practices invites struggles in our communities about what we want from our schools and our children. We must ask what the purposes of education are, and from there we are led into questions about what kind of society the schools that we have are creating. These are hard and contentious questions, but exciting ones. We should welcome them. If we hope to take advantage of this period of rich school reform research and a national focus on education we must ask hard questions about the way we use time and money, and look carefully at the answers.

Ultimately, communities have the right and indeed the responsibility to oversee the local schools. Of course, multiple forces at the federal, state, and local levels determine to a great extent what happens in schools and how it happens. However, school discussions often sound as if school policy and priorities were on the third tablet handed to Moses. Budget categories are fixed, time schedules are rigidly adhered to, even though they feature starting times that are way too early for any learning and ending times that leave children with long afternoons alone.

Along with acknowledging that change is indeed necessary, we have to accept our own responsibility for that change. Too often change is seen as something that the "school system" does. Parents are rarely involved in designing and implementing a change process, and when things look "different" in the classroom, angry questions often begin to fly. School board members rarely have the time and opportunity to study in depth research findings on which school-change proposals are based and as a result often block reform at the board level. This book gives interested community members—from parents to teachers to school board members to leaders of community and business organizations—the tools and frameworks needed to participate in or even initiate a change process within their community in an authentic and collaborative way.

"Put up or shut up" was one of my mother's favorite sayings, even though she was always a bit embarrassed to be saying the words "shut up." The aphorism was updated and reworked a bit in the sixties to "Either you're part of the solution or you're part of the problem." These sayings are a warning to anyone advocating a new reform idea in education. Avalanches of national reports and recommendations for school change have sounded the clarion call for better schools, through increased parental involvement, higher standards, increased homework, voucher plans, charter schools, full community schools, authentic assessment—and the list goes on. National organizations, funded by millions of federal government and foundation dollars, have been built around particular approaches to school reform and restructuring. School boards are asked to evaluate slickly packaged promotional materials as salesmen sweet-talk their way into the hearts and minds of teachers. I suspect that the market for educational ideas and programs to solve education's ills exceeds that for diet foods and fads!

Genuine educational philosophers I admire and agree with tell us that teachers should care more, schools should be communities, and students must have authentic learning experiences. All excellent advice—but advice that can't be effective unless the daily routines of school change. And despite pockets of educational experimentation around the country, little changes for the vast majority of students in our public schools where the fundamental structures of schooling remain remarkably the same as they were fifty years ago.[1] Bells ring all too often, students move in groups, textbooks drive the construction of school knowledge, and students cram for tests and forget the material the next day.

Schools That Do Too Much was written to help us sort through the national barrage of research and recommendations on school change by providing new conceptual lenses to process what we are seeing. It tries to tabulate the irrational aspects of how school days are structured. It provides some basic information about how school budgets are formed and presents a model for constructive community involvement in schools. Some of the recommendations included may seem radical on first hearing. Like calls for the end of homework, the suggestion to move sports out of the domain of public schools may send shock waves through many communities. But after the initial shock, we begin to wonder, Why do high schools sponsor competitive sports programs? What else do we do in a school that seems out of keeping with twenty-first-century educational goals?

Schools That Do Too Much differs from other school reform books in that it focuses on the prerequisites to any authentic change—rethinking how time and money are spent. There are two other differences as well. First, it argues for placing real responsibility for school reform beyond the schoolhouse walls. Too often, business as usual for our schools means that they must pick up the pieces for fragmented community life. This will not produce the kinds of learning results we are looking for. Communities must work together to lighten the load of schools that have been charged with doing too much.

It is not the case that there is no community involvement in schools; the problem is that community involvement in schools is often misdirected. Community leaders form well-publicized committees to help schools improve, but sadly, information usually flows one way: from the community to the schools. Business leaders tell school leaders what skills they need their future employees to possess, and they suggest solutions to school problems that come from the world of business. Sometimes CEOs even read a story to first-graders—and, incidentally, get lots of free press for their time. It is rare, however, to hear any of these community leaders begin by asking questions: What can we do to help? How can we lighten your burden? Community leaders need to look at their own cultures and practices and see how they can take over some of the responsibilities we currently push off on the schools. *Schools That Do Too Much* explores why this shift is needed and how it can happen.

Another difference between this book and others on school reform is that I look at the issue of standards from a new perspective. Many worry that standards-based education—in which curricula and assessment are guided by agreed-upon standards arrived at on the state or national level—will continue to be used as a justification for high-stakes testing and one-size-fits-all educational reform. The appropriation of the standards movement by advocates of increased testing is unfortunate. Setting educational standards does not automatically mean high-stakes testing. I argue that the real value of standards is to help communities make decisions about how to use scarce educational resources. Education standards could provide a framework to help schools and communities talk about increasing academic achievement and the resources needed to achieve the desired results.

The research for this book began on my first day of teaching, over thirty years ago. Since that time, I have spent countless thousands of hours in schools as both a teacher and a teacher educator. I have visited schools in this country and around the world as an educational consultant and have served in them as a Fulbright scholar. My research agenda was shaped by the questions that have grown out of my experiences as an educator, and they all relate to one fundamental question: How do we rid our schools of the activities and programs that interfere with children's ability to make use of the school day for authentic and systematic learning? From this question comes a whole series of rarely asked questions:

- Is it possible to link the resources of time and money to the education standards we have set for our children?
- Are there ways to talk about time use in schools beyond the typical "time on task" language of most educational research?
- Is it possible to uncover the relationship between the way we spend time in school and the way we allocate money in the school budget?
- How can we recalibrate the relationship between schools and communities so that schools shoulder less of the burden for the upbringing of America's children?

I wanted to know whether the stories I was hearing around the country squared with research on time use in schools. Did the claims parents were making about the way money was allocated in schools match the line items in school budgets? This book is in part an attempt to give a "public microphone" to the parents and teachers I have worked with over the years and to answer their questions.

My research associate, Chelsea Mooser, conducted extended on-site classroom visitations in schools as a way to verify the claims we were hearing from parents and teachers. I have had a number of school administrators, teachers, and students read various parts of the manuscript in order to ensure that I "have it right" when I describe the school day.

The site studies corroborated what I knew from my own experiences as a teacher, from research findings, and from what I heard around the country: the school day in the United States is chaotic, truncated, and not designed to be conducive to real learning. In addition, what are called by many educators the "sideshows of education" consume a far greater amount of time and energy than they warrant, a finding supported by important research, as we shall see.

Alexandra, whose school day I describe in chapter 1, is a composite of students I know well. The details of her time in school have been drawn from actual on-site investigations conducted by my research associate. The stories about school issues that are sprinkled throughout the book are actual school events that I have experienced as a teacher or a researcher.

A word about writing about schools. Those of us who write about schools must walk a fine line between what is perceived by some as school bashing and trying to tell it like it is. To suggest that there are problems with the way we use time and money in schools and that we should look at these issues is not to denigrate our teachers and administrators.

In fact, administrators and teachers are the ones who have brought many of the issues raised in this book to my attention. The insights and recommendations in the book have come in part from teachers and principals who have brought to my attention certain impediments to learning—as well as ways to eliminate them. Most teachers are as concerned about these barriers to learning as I am. They often contend that their local school boards make decisions that are counterproductive. Community pressure for big sports programs, parents who take their kids on vacations during the school year, and social programs in the school all eat away at the time devoted to core academic learning. Teachers and administrators know it, but are hardpressed to change these ways of "doing school." *Schools That Do Too Much* examines these issues in order to help schools prioritize their activities.

Furthermore, the fact that I make some general statements about schools should not be taken to mean that I think all schools are the same. There is tremendous variation in the structure and form of schools today. Thanks in part to the reform movement and the courage of educators to build "break-the-mold schools," many schools in this country are trying to do things differently. Some of these schools have had a tremendous impact on the lives of children and on our knowledge about what works. You will find reference to these success stories throughout the book and in the "Suggested Readings" section at the end.

Finally, the recommendations in this book are not meant to suggest that we shouldn't increase funding for education, lower class size significantly, and provide all children with prekindergarten education. These recommendations—some of them resulted from a recent Rand Corporation study—are fundamental to improved educational outcomes in this country. At the same time, however, I argue that we need the strength to critique the existing daily structures that determine the quality of life in our classrooms.

In chapter 1 I look into the typical day of a high school junior, and analyze the ways in which time is spent and misspent in the daily routine of the American school. Chapter 2 is about the structure of the school day; here I examine the history of the school schedule and some of the historical factors that determined the modern school day, as well as features of this historical moment that point to the possibility of change. Chapter 3 takes a close look at school budgets: How do budgeting processes, by complication and obfuscation, impede our ability to understand how our schools spend their dollars? How can understanding the history of school budgeting give us a broader perspective outside our own narrow interests as parents or teachers? And what can we do about it? A "school budgets for dummies" section presents a step-by-step guide to mastering the budgeting process. In chapter 4 I take aim at the single most disruptive school program: competitive after-school athletics. How did sports became housed in public schools in this country and what is its impact on the learning environment in schools? This chapter unpacks the way school budgets misrepresent the full time and money expense of sports programs.

Part II turns the critical lessons of Part I into recommendations designed to improve learning. In chapter 5 we explore alternative approaches to budgeting, especially the concept of zero-based budgeting, a kind of financial starting from scratch. I lay out principles and steps that must underlie an open, zero-based budgeting exercise in any community. Chapter 6 focuses on that other scarce resource, time, as we explore a new paradigm for organizing the school day based on results of experiments from around the country, as well as a host of other recommendations for unburdening the school. These practical suggestions present ways for schools and communities to re-focus their schools on learning. In the concluding chapter I suggest a new metaphor for schooling: the "school as sacred space." What would a classroom treated as sacred space look like? Thinking of schools as sacred space will help us sort out what belongs in school and what needs to be done elsewhere in the community. The school as sa-cred space sends a clear message that the days are past when we asked schools to be all things to all people. Now we must concentrate on the core purposes to which schools should be dedicated.

Part I

CHAPTER 1

The Fractured School Day:
Competing Interests,
Competing Priorities

Once we know that some youngsters receive as little
as eighteen minutes of instruction per hour . . . what
does the researcher who made the startling announcement do for an encore?

—Philip W. Jackson

*A*s Alexandra drives onto the grounds of Willard High School she
notices that her soccer team's game tomorrow with rival Wilson
High is listed on the Willard bulletin board. This board is the pride of
the community, a large, well-lit structure that the town spent three
years raising money for and two years fighting with the planning
commission to build. It helps keep the town informed about events at
the school. Today it announces the wrestling team's meet, Alexandra's
soccer meet, and the junior varsity football game tonight. The school
play that Alexandra's best friend is starring in is not listed; Alexandra
makes a mental note to say something to someone about that, and
picks up her speed in order to make the first bell, which rings at 7:28.
Alexandra mounts the steps as her fellow students struggle into their
first-period class to beat the final bell, which rings four minutes later.
Some of these students have been up since 6:15 getting ready for and
getting themselves to school; others look as though they just crawled

out of bed. Alexandra began her day with a swim practice from 5:15–
to 6:00 and hurried home to get ready for school, so unlike that of
some of her classmates, her day was well under way by 7:28.

The crackling of the loudspeaker signals the official opening of the
school day at Willard High School. In an uneven voice, the student of
the day leads the whole school in the flag salute, and then various students who have lined up outside the front office announce the events
of importance that day. Team practice times, bus departure times
for sports teams and fan buses, makeup exam schedules, due dates for
the junior raffle tickets, club meeting places and postponements, reminders of popular students' birthdays, and a singing of "Happy
Birthday" for . . . well, someone; no one quite knows because the student who is leading the song is laughing so hard the name of the hon-
ored person is inaudible. Alexandra, a driven young woman who has
her sights set on life after high school, is a bit bored by the whole routine and has little use for the students who participate in the daily ritual at Willard. By 7:39, the flag salute over and the speaker quiet, the
teacher begins to pick up where the class left off the day before.

"When you read the last half of the chapter last night did anything
strike you about the similarities between the Hayes versus Tilden election and last year's election in this country?"

A few hands shoot up. Even though this is an honors-level history
class, many students slide to the back of the room and spend most of
each period trying to wake up. Of those awake, about half have kept up
with the reading, and it is these students' hands that wave eagerly in
front of the teacher.

At 7:40 a bell sounds in the distance, signaling the start of physical
education classes. The PE bell breaks Alexandra's concentration; she
had just formulated a solid answer to the teacher's question, but the
bell reminded her that she left her PE locker unlocked last night and
she hoped that all her stuff would still be there today.

For sixteen minutes, the history class continues uninterrupted. At
7:55, the door opens and the office aid enters to collect the roll sheets.
Since the teacher has forgotten to take roll that day, she quickly asks
who is missing, which turns into a group activity of "Where's Celine?"
"Who has seen Martin?"

After the roll-taking interlude of four minutes, focus is reestablished for two minutes, until the PE bell rings in the distance again. This bell signals the end of the PE class, which gives PE students twelve minutes to take a shower and get ready for their next class. For many students in the history class, this bell is the relief bell, signaling to them that the class is almost over and that they have survived another period of not being called on for answers they don't have.

Alexandra's day is divided into forty-two-minute class periods, so the bell signaling the end of class rings at 8:14. Students have four minutes to change classes and for those four minutes all hell breaks loose as students hurry to classes and grab new books from their lockers, couples steal kisses in the hallway, and unsettled scores are resolved with quick shoves and threats of retribution. Alexandra hurries to her English class, stopping in the bathroom, where there is a long line. She makes a quick calculation and realizes that she won't make it to a stall before the final bell rings; she leaves the bathroom, vowing to get a hall pass during her next class. By the time the final bell rings most students are in their classes. Period 2 begins at 8:18.

The flurry of activity between classes means that it takes the students in Alexandra's English class awhile to settle down. As the teacher takes roll, students remark to each other about who is wearing what, who has dyed her hair the night before, and who is holding hands with whom.

In Alexandra's English class, students are presenting their group projects on Joseph Conrad's *Heart of Darkness*. Each day for a week and a half, the teacher has been drawing the name of a group that will be the first to present for that day. Today, the first group for the day is assembled in front of the class by 8:23 and is ready to begin. Three minutes into their presentation, the PE bell again rings in the distance.

And at 8:32 the loudspeaker crackles on and the office secretary says, "Sorry for the interruption, but would Mr. Mares please come to the office."

The first group presentation is completed by 8:39 and the second group is in front of the class and ready to begin by 8:45. As they begin, the PE rings in the background and Alexandra sinks into her seat and appears to be thinking, "Saved by the bell." The second group ends a bit early, so students sit and talk quietly with their friends until the passing bell rings at 9:00.

Students have a fifteen-minute locker break until 9:15. Alexandra tries again to make it to the bathroom. This time the line is longer. Alexandra waits and talks to a friend on the swim team who is complaining about what the chlorine is doing to her hair. Alexandra looks at her own hair and is thankful that she has her mother's thick, curly hair, which seems immune to chlorine damage. The bell rings to call the students to period 3, but Alexandra is next in line. At first she thinks she will wait it out, but when two minutes pass she realizes that she will have to get a pass from her next class and try again. She runs to class and slides in just as the final bell rings, only to remember that today is the day her ecology paper is due and it is still in her locker.

The teacher calls the class to order, reminding students that their papers are due today; a number of students are in Alexandra's predicament of having to ask to go to their lockers to get their papers. Mr. Parker is visibly disturbed by the fact that well over a third of the students didn't remember to bring their papers with them this day. He tells them that they can bring their papers in during lunch because he wants to begin a new unit today on water quality and doesn't want to lose all the time it would take for them to go and come back. Roll is taken and four minutes into the class period, Mr. Parker has captured everyone's attention with a vial of very dirty water that he has collected from the very pool where the swim team practices.

During the forty-two-minute class, two PE bells, the attendance taker, and a representative from student government who is delivering a questionnaire about the upcoming dance interrupt the class. The student asks Mr. Parker if he would mind having his period 6 students answer the questionnaires and assures him it will only take a few minutes. Absent-mindedly, Mr. Parker agrees and puts the pile of questionnaires on top of the other pile of papers on his desk and tries to get back to the water in the vial, which still has the student's attention. He has enhanced the lesson with a computerized overhead that is showing the chemical makeup of swimming-pool water. Luckily, Mr. Parker's subject for the day and his cool computerized projections have kept student attention focused on the subject at hand, notwithstanding the fact that during his forty-two-minute period, a full twelve minutes were taken up with interruptions and time needed to refocus. Mr. Parker's most common expression is "Where were we?"

Period 4, Alexandra's math class, is a welcome break from the other classes. All the students have their own computers and are working on individualized programs in pre-calculus. The teacher moves from student to student, troubleshooting, helping answer questions, and directing students' attention to their mistakes. Toward the end of the period the loudspeaker comes on to remind sophomores that today is AIDS education day and they are all to report to their groups for period 7. For this semester, the entire tenth-grade class spends one class period a week in AIDS education groups led by teachers who have received intense training in a nationwide program.

Few students in the math class seem to notice that there is an announcement on. Alexandra seems to have developed the ability to listen for key words from the loudspeaker and listens only when she hears something that pertains to her. All the students in this class are juniors or seniors, and they all seem to be tuning out simultaneously.

Alexandra has "first lunch," the first scheduled lunch period. It is a forty-two-minute feeding frenzy in a chaotic cafeteria with little air and less natural light. Today, Alexandra spends her lunch period with her friends; on other days she goes straight to the library to catch up on homework. Today they laugh about their friend Martha, who has her first boyfriend and who now spends her time in the hallway with him. The three girls on the swim team who are also in the ecology class talk about the water in the swimming pool and realize that the reason that Adriana is having so much trouble with her hair is that she has recently bleached it and the chemicals in the bleach have reacted negatively with the chemicals in the pool water. Since Mr. Parker announced that they would have to do an ecology project this semester Adriana tries to talk the rest of the girls into doing the project on her hair. This discussion reminds them that they have to get their papers to Mr. Parker during lunch, so Alexandra quickly packs up and is off to turn her ecology paper in before she goes to her sixth-period art class.

Period 6 begins with midday announcements. Since the art class is next to the cafeteria, the voice of the secretary making the announcements has to compete with the noise from second lunch as she tells the wrestling team that their match has been canceled. Everyone in the art room is asking everyone else what has just been said. No one much cares when they hear the words "wrestling," since only six students in the whole school are on the wrestling team, but a full four minutes of period 6 has been taken up with news of the wrestling team. Alexandra's art project, a series of self-portraits, is just completed; all that is left is to do the final shading and then she can hang them in the student gallery. Since all students in the state must take an art elective, the class is overcrowded with students and art projects. Today a number of students are absent, but there are still twenty-six. Masks are hung from the ceiling; collages are stacked up all over; the ceiling tiles are being painted by one student as a project. Glue, paste, scissors, wire cutters, wood scrapes, flat files, and piles of papier-mâché figures lie around. Some students are working hard; others sit clustered around work tables talking softly and avoiding the work at hand. Alexandra is a bit put off by the classroom—annoyed by the noise in the room, the lack of respect of some of the students for art, and the general chaos. The teacher is a favorite of many students and since many students are on their lunch break, they wander in and out of the art classroom at will. Alexandra is certain that she could have finished the project long ago if it hadn't been for the interruptions and disorder in the classroom. She asks students at the next table to turn down their Walkman. Even though they are listening through headphones, the music is so loud that Alexandra can hear the driving beat of music she hates. They tell her to "chill out," and she turns her back to them, trying to get some peace. As the class settles down, Alexandra and the other students begin some serious work and for eight minutes the art class is a delightful art studio with students working hard. The loudspeaker interrupts the hard-won concentration with a reminder about the student government questionnaires on the upcoming dance. The teacher's attention, which had been focused fully on one student's project, is drawn to the loudspeaker.

"Did anyone hear what they said?"

"Yea," yells a student, "something about questions about a dance."

"Who cares?" yells another.

Alexandra knows what was said, but prefers to focus down even harder on her art piece instead of answering the questions.

A questionnaire shows up on Alexandra's table, so she knows that the teacher has figured out what he was asked to do. The rest of the period is lost to students talking about the questionnaire and the dance and the last dance and the car accident that happened after the last dance and the music that sucked at the last dance and the new school policy about not being able to leave dances once you enter. And on and on until the passing bell rings.

Period 7, Alexandra's PE class, is designed to be the warm-up period for the girl's soccer team. The class time flows naturally into the after-school team practice. Today during the class period they watch a video of the last game and talk about the upcoming game with an archrival. For some reason there are no loudspeakers in the gym or team rooms, so the class period is not interrupted by the end-of-the-school-day announcements. The practice officially begins as the final bell of the school day rings. For two and a half hours the girls focus intensely on their practice. No bells ring, there are no attendance takers interrupting the coach, the loudspeaker never draws the attention of the students and coaches away from the task at hand. There are nineteen girls on the team and three coaches. The coaches break the girls into practice teams, work one on one with each girl on her individual strengths and weaknesses, and have small groups practice particular skills; today the groups are working on passing.

When Alexandra makes it home for the evening, it is 6:15. She has been on the go since her early-morning swim practice, giving her a solid thirteen-hour day. As she enters her room, she drops her thirty-two-pound backpack on the bed and begins to wonder whether she has everything she needs for her homework that night.

"I have a brain cramp," thinks Alexandra as she forgets her homework and heads for the kitchen to help with dinner.

What's Wrong with Alexandra's Day?

Alexandra's day—punctuated by bells, interruptions, and non-essential activities that crowd out opportunities for real learning—could be "any day, any school, U.S.A." Unfortunately, the fractured, chaotic school day is common in this country—the norm rather than the exception.

Simply cataloging the details of a typical day should cause a few eyebrows to rise, and make you think. Obviously some of the chaos, the frenetic pace, is inevitable. School is a lively, densely scheduled place, no matter how you organize it. Any building where children outnumber adults by dozens to one is bound to be busy, even crazy sometimes. But I want to argue that the typical waste of time in schools goes far beyond what's necessary. The schedule of a typical school day in this country is under our control. In fact, schedules are structured the way they are to serve specific interests and specific priorities. I believe we need to change those priorities.

So what's really wrong? First the specifics.

Alexandra's day starts much too early. Recent research suggests that adolescents don't really wake up until around 9 A.M.

Bells ring almost continually. During each class period, the bell rings once to start the class; the PE bell rings twice, once eight minutes into each class and again twelve minutes before the end of each class; the passing bell rings to signal the end of class. That is four bells during a forty-two-minute class period!

And the loudspeaker! Controlled by the front office, the loudspeaker can break into classroom time whenever front-office staff decide to do so; they might consider a parent's request to deliver a forgotten lunch reason enough to disrupt the entire school. In addition, the loudspeaker announcements often define an "in-crowd" set of activities that has the effect of distancing students whose birthdays are not being celebrated by the whole school and students whose extracurricular activities are never the subject of loudspeaker announcements.

Taking roll each period and having students coming into class to collect the completed roll sheets eats up far too much time and disrupts valuable learning time. Unless teachers have students sit in assigned seats, roll taking can consume up to four minutes, and as class sizes increase, teachers are spending more time just taking attendance.

Forty-two-minute periods are too short to do much with, and have the further effect of cutting the school day into bite-size pieces of time. Many high schools have moved to block schedules so class time is over eighty minutes rather than forty-two. This change cuts transition time in half, but by itself does little to rationalize the school day, as I shall show later.

Well-intentioned stand-alone programs that are not part of the academic program eat up valuable time. Essential as it is that students be educated about AIDS, we should ask whether AIDS education should be more than part of a solid health education program.

There are two patterns of wasted time that run through this fragmented, chaotic school day. First, the flow of the entire school day that surrounds each class period creates unnecessary waste and puts too much pressure on the individual class periods. And second, the chaotic nature of life in the classroom wastes the learning time available within the class period itself.

First consider the overall day. The day starts and ends too early. The flow of the school day is broken into fragments that are punctuated by odd time divisions. The irony of this minute-by-minute carving up of the school day is that it gives the appearance of using time effectively, when in fact, time is wasted flagrantly. In some high schools there are ten periods, which means a full fifty minutes each day is spent *just* in moving from class to class. Researchers have found that at the high school level, 15 percent of the school day is spent in transition time as students move from class to class.[1]

Classroom life itself becomes even more fragmented because of the interruptions by the bells and loudspeaker, not to mention the roll takers' coming and going, which further disrupts concentrated learning. Researchers have found that transition time within the classroom can account for up to 38 percent of the class period.[2] So in a forty-two-minute period, close to twenty minutes can be consumed by taking the roll, collecting homework, giving out assignments for the next day, and setting up group work. Time is lost in packing and unpacking for each class. At the high school level, it is quite typical for the first five minutes of each class to be used getting ready to start class and the last five minutes, for getting ready to change classes. If there are ten periods, that adds an hour and forty minutes to "transition time." Added to the fifty minutes for passing time, and you get high school students spending a full two hours each day in moving from class to class!

Of course it is not possible to have school without transitions and "down time." The issue is how much of this time is a necessary part of any learning day and how much is time wasted by the use of structures and practices that need to be changed.

Whose Interests?

The fractured school day did not just happen, nor is the time schedule for public schools set in stone. Most of us haven't thought much about what priorities are embedded in the ways that we structure our school days. Whose interests are being met by school's ending at 1:20? Why do the bells ring at odd times? Why do front-office workers have the ability to override classroom instruction with loudspeaker announcements?

We don't often ask these questions because many of these practices and structures are inherited as part of the culture of schools. These ways of doing things in schools are seen as business as usual. But we should be asking our school boards, school administrators, and ourselves these hard questions. Ask a school board member about the shape of the school day, and you are likely to hear all kinds of reasons why the teachers' and other unions have set the time schedules the way they have. What school administrators are less willing to admit is that the schedule meets the needs of the competitive athletic program and always has. Even in communities whose schools no longer offer after-school sports programs, the schedule is the same as it was when the school did in fact offer sports. (This particular point will be developed extensively in chapter 4.)

In this traditional, accepted structure, the school day ends in the early afternoon, in some schools as early as 1:20! This time frame leaves long afternoons for sports practice. Since most students do not participate in competitive athletic programs after school, many communities must struggle to find meaningful activities for students for this chunk of time. What is the message that we are sending when we reserve the best part of the day for sports? With sports embedded in the public-school system and administrators often coming up through the ranks of coaches and athletic directors, who will raise the question of whether classroom time should be interrupted by announcements about "router" buses and practice times and pep assemblies? If we put student learning at the center of our thinking and our planning in schools, then these administrative activities become secondary to the learning needs of kids.

And what about the nature of time within the classroom? Whose interests are served by the disruptions and fragmented time schedule? No one doubts that having hundreds and sometimes thousands of students in a school building is an administrative nightmare. Certainly we need to know where the kids are at all times, we need to be certain that there is fairness in the way time gets divided, and we need to ensure the community that we are in control of the time the students are at school. But these administrative duties have become the driving priorities of the school. Making sure that everyone is in their place has overtaken making sure that every one is learning. Bells, loudspeakers, roll takers, and the like are all administrative functions that appear to have acquired a higher priority than learning.

The real issue is whether academic learning time should be foregone for "the sideshows of education." For many teachers the line in the sand—the most important issue—is the length of the class period; they know that class time is the least sacred commodity in the school and is encroached on by sports-related events in the form of loudspeaker announcements, by parents in the form of deliveries of forgotten lunches, and by "the system" in the form of roll takers and compliance announcements over the loudspeaker.

Some readers may respond, "Well, in my school we have much longer periods, eighty minutes." These longer periods do indeed help diminish the chaos of the school day and have been a central feature of the reform of the use of time in schools. In fact, I will discuss the issue of alternative class schedules in a later chapter. But by itself, lengthening the class period will not create the new culture that is needed in schools. Nor does the longer class period really address the central issue that we face when looking at the truncated, fractured school day: Namely, what does the way we use time tell us about the priorities we have set for our schools? Beleaguered teachers will often say that it seems that student learning is the last thing on anyone's mind during the school day, not to mention when the school day and year are being planned. By looking at the way we structure time use in schools, we might all agree!

A Brief History of Time Analysis in School

How can we think productively and systematically about what's wrong with the way time is spent in schools and what to do about it?

Researchers trying to determine how best to understand the way time gets used in school have developed useful categories that distinguish between different types of time use and that help point the way to new ways to think about this issue.

Researchers draw an important distinction between instructional time and the total amount of time spent in school. Instructional time measures of the amount of time per day students spend exposed to instruction in their classes. Amount of time in school is a measure of the length of the school day. Alexandra's instructional time was four hours and fifty-four minutes, and the time she spent in school was nine hours and fifteen minutes—but let's remember that two hours and three minutes of that time was spent in very intense, uninterrupted instruction in soccer. This left a total of one hour and fifteen minutes that was not instructional and not soccer.

The average instructional time in the United States for high school students is five hours and thirty minutes,[3] and the average amount of time students in the United States spend in school is six hours and twenty minutes.[4] Averages in the United States are not far from Alexandra's actual experience, given the fact that close to three hours of the time that Alexandra spends in school is spent in an after-school athletic program.

This rather crude distinction between instructional time and total time does not, however, really help us understand the nuances of the school day. For the past fifty years, researchers have struggled to find ways to refine their understanding of the use of time in schools.

The efficiency movement of the fifties found researchers in classrooms with stopwatches. The focus of this research was to count the specific teacher and student behaviors and then to relate these behaviors to measures of student achievement. These studies, called "time-on-task," broke the complex interactions of teaching and learning into discrete "pieces" of information. There were a number of problems with this line of research. For one, it was premised on a very simplistic notion of learning. We now know that learning is not a one-way street. Teachers may be standing in front of a class lecturing, students may be sitting at desks with pencils in hand, but those task activities do not tell us what is going on in the head of the student or in their hearts. Another problem with this research method was the lack of sophistication in the instruments used to measure what is a very complex set of interactions in the ecology of the teacher-student-environment when it comes to learning. Is the fact that a teacher is standing in front of the class instructing in fraction multiplication a real marker of learning?

By the 1970s researchers developed more elaborate categories for studying the use of classroom time. In part because quality of time was seen as increasingly important in educational reform, researchers developed a variety of terms to describe just how students were using the time they did have. Researchers clocked allocated time, engaged time, and academic learning time. In this research format, allocated time was the time set aside for teaching a particular subject. Engaged time was the time students were actually working on that particular subject, allowing us to draw a distinction between the allocated time for learning and the time learning might actually be going on.

There is always a gap between allocated time and engaged time. The gap includes the time it takes for a class to settle into the work of the subject. For instance, there is a period called "transition time," when students are settling into the class or getting ready to move to the next one. Transition time can take up to ten minutes at each end of a class. This can mean that out of a sixty-minute reading class, there are actually only forty minutes available for engaged time. Researchers' best efforts aside, accurately determining "engaged time" would really require a mind reader. Even the best researchers would have a hard time telling whether Alexandra is actually experiencing "engaged time" when she is looking intently at her ecology teacher.

And finally, academic learning time is a measure of the time when the balance was perfect for learning. Defined as the amount of time students spend performing relevant academic tasks with a high level of success, academic learning time measures are a pretty good predictor of student achievement.[5] Academic learning time is a slightly arcane mathematical calculation that measures types of learning activities according to level of difficulty of material measured against a student's ability to work with the material. This figure is designed to capture the magical moment in learning when students are working on material that is not too hard, not too easy, but just right for learning to occur.[6] This research has yielded a number of interesting findings.

Looking in classrooms for over a year, researchers found that although sixty minutes might be allocated to reading instruction during a particular day, a mere twenty-four minutes were actual academic learning time. Over the course of a 150-day school year in one particular class studied, there were 120 hours of engaged time, but only half of that time, sixty hours, was academic learning time.[7]

So for Alexandra, the allocated time for science was forty-two minutes. The engaged time was less. If you remember, she lost twelve minutes in that class to interruptions; we are down to thirty minutes of engaged time. In this particular class, Alexandra's academic learning time was probably pretty high since the lesson had to do with the a subject close to her heart, the pollution levels in the swimming pool.

Let's look back at Alexandra's full day using these terms. Her amount of time in school was nine hours and fifteen minutes, including the after-school soccer practice. She has seven periods, each forty-two minutes so she has four hours and fifty-four minutes of allocated time. But what about engaged time? Should we count the twenty-six minutes that she spent listening to the student reports on *Heart of Darkness*—filled with glaring historical errors and a very weak definition of imperialism—as engaged time? What about the forty-two minutes she spent warming up in PE? Most of us agree that that time should not be counted as engaged time. That means that although Alexandra spent nine hours and fifteen minutes in school (including her sports practice) her total academic learning time had to be something significantly less than four hours and twelve minutes; it is likely, given the evidence of research, that her academic learning time was even just half of that time, or roughly two hours.

What is perhaps most remarkable about Alexandra's day is that for a full three hours and fifteen minutes she had a perfect learning environment. No interruptions, a student teacher ratio of one to six, and pedagogical practices that build on an adolescent's developmental need to belong. Was this her math class? Her English class? Her science class? Was this time turned over to intense individual work? Did she work on her intellectual passion for writing a play? Nope, she played sports. For which she will be rewarded—she hopes—with a big, fat college scholarship, and her name on the front page of the local newspaper and in lights on the Willard bulletin board if her team wins the state championship.

I will argue that the huge investment that some schools make in sports reflects a misplaced priority. But on the other hand, I believe we can learn a lot about how to reorganize the academic day by looking at the kinds of environments children thrive in from looking at sports. This will be discussed further in Part II.

Instructional Time and the Lower Grades

At the elementary level, the erosion of learning time looks a bit different. Researchers generally acknowledge that up to 25 percent of time in the elementary classroom is spent in transition time.[8] This time includes transition activities from subject to subject, and time spent regrouping and handing in homework and the like. Individual students can waste enormous amounts of time by trying to distract the teacher, sitting with their hands up waiting for individual help and going back and forth to the bathroom. These are daily regularities of classroom life. Many suggest that they are alterable by means of im-proved classroom management techniques, which is no doubt true to a certain extent, but some of this time is, simply, much-needed "downtime" in a very fast-paced school day.

Managing the demands of a room full of energetic and often needy students takes tremendous energy by all the players in the classroom.

But beyond the necessary time constraints within the life of an ele-mentary classroom, communities have tremendous expectations for their elementary schools. These expectations, often implicit, deter-mine to a great extend how time is used in the elementary school. It is in the host of activities that crowd the elementary school day that a community's priorities and values for their schools are made explicit. For example, in many schools children are pulled from their class-rooms to participate in a months-long drug-awareness program con-ducted by police officers who come into the school. We probably all agree that drug awareness is important for our children to learn—but have we ever looked at the costs in lost learning time that these kinds of programs represent?

Parents have a strong desire to be involved in the school in significant ways, yet most of us would be surprised to know how much instructional time is turned over to activities that are only tangentially related to academic learning. For example, full afternoons can be lost because parents hold birthday parties for their children at school. Fund-raising activities in the upper grades can consume energy and time as students are asked to raise the money needed for end-of-the year trips. Principals bemoan the time that teachers spend getting ready and celebrating holidays—making paper turkeys for Thanksgiving and May baskets in the spring.

School people believe that it is the community that wants sports programs, drug education in the schools, and Halloween parades during the school day. If this is true, perhaps it is time for our communities to begin conversations about the educational value of eighth-graders selling wrapping paper to pay for trips to Disneyland.

Time: Quantity vs. Quality

There are only two fundamental ways that we think about improving time for instruction in schools. We can increase the quantity of time students spend in school, and we can improve the quality of the time that they spend in school. Some researchers suggest that increased time allotted to a subject does not always increase academic achievement.[9] And some go so far as to suggest that quality of time is more important than the quantity![10] This research suggests that increasing the length of the school day and the school year should be undertaken only after we improve the quality of time use in schools. Despite this, sheer quantity of time is the most discussed variable when talk turns to improving students' academic achievement.

Since the beginning of the twentieth century, the amount of time spent by students in school has increased steadily. In 1900 schools were in session an average of 143.7 days and students attended an average of 98 days. Now, the average school calendar is 180 days.[11] Extending the length of the school day and school year has been on the educational reform agenda since the publication of the influential 1984 report *A Nation at Risk*, published by the National Commission on Excellence in Education. The report, sometimes credited with sparking the current reform movement, detailed a deplorable state of public education in this country, comparing the purported crisis to an invading army on our shores. The report called for higher expectations, more content, and more time in school.[12] Whatever one thinks of the diagnoses of the report, the first two of its recommendations have been the subject of intense reform activities over the last 15 years. We have seen dramatic increases in academic standards; more required courses, and grade-level advancement based on test scores and not age levels. Increasing the school day to seven hours and the school year to 200 to 220 days has been the one recommendation made in *A Nation at Risk* that has languished. Few state legislatures have been able to increase the length of the school year, and in some states, battles over the schedule were so fierce that superintendents and board members were unseated.[13]

What has been apparent is that there are mighty forces working politically against lengthening the school year. The greatest obstacle is the staggering cost of the reform. According to one estimate, extending the school day to eight hours and the school year to 200 days would cost the United States more than $20 billion annually.[14] Parents have adopted a wait-and-see attitude toward the reform. Since Gallup began polling parents on their attitudes toward lengthening the school year and day, never have more than 50 percent of the respondents stated that it was a good idea. Owing in part to public resistance to longer school days and year, states and communities have been unable to shift the six-and-a-half-hour school day/180-day school year paradigm.

Rather than fighting to lengthen the school year, some schools are moving to year-round calendars as a way—advocates argue—to increase the quality of time available to teachers. This reform strategy most often centers on redistributing the existing 180-day school year rather than lengthening the school year and increasing costs. In this formulation, the 180 instructional days are broken into blocks. The "45/15" plan has four nine-week quarters (or 45 school days) separated by three-week intersessions. A "60/20" plan divides the school year into three terms, each twelve weeks, or sixty days, long with four-week breaks in between. Some schools use the intersession time to give remedial instruction to students, which has the effect of lengthening the school year.

The year-round schools help solve one problem: "fall review." We all remember returning to school in the fall. We had to write essays on what we'd done over the summer vacation, and there were the shifting classes and teachers until we were set up "right" in our reading groups and math groups. Then there was the literal review of material from the previous semester, which so many of us had forgotten over the long summer. And finally there was the adjustment period for students as they learned how to work with a particular teacher. Researchers suggest that this fall period of adjustment is long and inefficient.[15] By shortening the intersession periods, part of the inevitable loss is avoided. No one has yet to calculate how much time is lost as teachers learn a new group of students each year. But just making decisions about new student groupings typically confines a group of teachers to poring over student folders for a good two weeks at the end of each school year. The problem of fall review has led some to break the mold and structure their programs so that teachers work with the same group of students over the course of three or four years.

Generally, though, there is little evidence that year-round schools increase aggregate student learning, although students from economically disadvantaged, non-English- speaking homes do seem to benefit from year-round schools in terms of learning increases.[16] (We will come back to some of these alternative time strategies in Part II.)

Whatever the marginal benefits of year-round schedules in eliminating some problems related to fall review, there is a lot more to the time issue than that. When we shift our attention from quantity to quality of time, a whole different set of questions arises. Is grouping students by age and ability the most effective organizational structure for learning? Is moving students from teacher to teacher each year best for student learning? Are forty-two-minute time blocks the best for learning? And what about time spent in core and noncore subjects? These are typical of the questions that capture our attention when we turn our attention to quality-of-time issues in school.

Concerned in part with poor U.S. showings on international test-score comparisons, Congress passed the Education Council Act of 1991, which established Public Law 102–62. This law mandated the establishment of the commission, which was charged with conducting a comprehensive review of the relationship between time and learning in the nation's schools. Composed of a mix of educators, politicians and community leaders, the commission spent twenty-four months visiting schools, holding formal hearings, conducting overseas fact-finding trips to Japan and Germany. This is the most comprehensive look at the issue of time in schools in the past fifty years, and provides a troubling picture of schooling today: with few exceptions, the school day starts at 7:30 and ends at 2:15; the school day is six periods which last 51 minutes (the national average); the school year is nine months; high school graduation is based on seat-time; and secondary-school students spend only 41 percent of the day on core academic subjects.[17]

In order to measure quality of time use in schools, researchers need to spend an enormous amount of time in schools; only this will give them a fuller understanding of the daily routines that work against even the best teachers and the subtle distinctions between time used well and time just used. Many researchers have been able to capture aspects of the culture of schools, but few have had the insights of Ernest Boyer about the impact of the chaotic school day. In his classic mid-eighties study of high schools, *High Schools: A Report on Secondary Education in America,* Boyer takes us inside classrooms and schools. He devotes almost two chapters to the use of time in schools and concludes:

> Our school visits convinced us that lengthening the school year is not a top priority for school reform. The urgent need is not more time but better use of time. The great problem today appears to be the incessant interruption of the bell, the constant movement of students from room to room; the feeling that the class is over just as learning has begun. There is not sufficient time to set up and complete science laboratory experiments, no time to write essays and critique them, and no time to engage in extended foreign language conversation.[18]

The problem of how to reorganize the day is one we will return to in Part II. For now, it is important to recognize that starting a public discussion about time use in schools must include a broad analysis and a discussion of priorities we have for our schools. Simply lengthening the school day or the school year without acknowledging that significant time is spent in activities only tangentially related to academic learning will not yield the kinds of results communities are looking for when they undertake a reform agenda.

In a moment that can stand as an ironic summary of the issue of quality of classroom time, Al Gore, during the 2000 presidential campaign, spoke to an honors-level history class in a Maine high school. That night on the national evening news we caught a few minutes of his teaching. In the background, we heard a voice over the loudspeaker requesting that a student come to the front office. I guess we could take comfort in the fact that even for the vice president schools do not turn off their loudspeakers!

I have argued so far that disruptions interfere with academic learning time in schools and that those disruptions can be traced to misplaced priorities. But there is another specific pressure on the structure of the school day, and merely changing the way time is organized won't fix it. An overcrowded, overextended curriculum and extracurricular program has made its way into American schools. Together, the poor-quality time and the extracurricular overload place unnecessary demands on schools, I believe, and they are a natural place to examine public priorities for education. We won't mend the way we spend time in school until we reexamine all the things we expect our schools to do.

CHAPTER 2

Who Could Be against Dental Health?: Defining the Mission of Schooling

*W*ho could be against dental health?" one veteran teacher asked her colleague as they entered the faculty meeting. When the school nurse presented her proposal to the teachers for a dental health program in the middle school, many teachers listened attentively. The program, part of a national effort to improve dental health in young people, had all the hallmarks of a good educational program. Lots of "hands-on/minds-on" activities, linking activities for the parents, an interdisciplinary curriculum that included art and nutrition as well as history and science. It even had a fun unit on careers in the field. Who could complain? The nurse assured the teachers that it would only take a total of twenty-five hours spread out over the course of a semester. The board member in attendance, a local dentist, talked to the teachers about his belief in the efficacy of such a program and the problems he was seeing in his office. When he finished, the principal called for questions.

The senior members of the staff were the first to speak. They wanted to know how they are to fit another "program" into their already jammed weekly schedule. One teacher asked if another program was going to be discontinued in order to make room for the dental health program. Another, not meaning to be cynical, asked if there were dental health questions on the eighth-grade exams. Newer members of the staff started to worry. They had yet to master the structure of the school day and the curriculum now in place—how could they add another program? Some commented that dental health was not included in the state learning standards so they couldn't spend time on it.

As the principal tried to navigate what was becoming a contentious discussion in front of a board member, the most senior member of the faculty rose. Connie was known to be one of the finest teachers in the state, a veteran who had had every honor bestowed on her that a teacher can get— master teacher status and twenty-five years of loyal parental support—to back up her words.

"I think the program sounds wonderful. You all know that I believe strongly in the education of the whole child and don't ever want to see the school curriculum just about the three R's. And I know I struggled with my own kids to get them to floss every night; I finally taught them to do it together in front of their favorite television show!"

The room broke into laughter as everyone imagined the floss in place next to the TV remote.

Connie continued, "My concern is that I don't see how we can fit this program into the school day. We talk informally all the time about how to make the school day less compressed and more focused. That can never happen if we keep adding programs that, while of great value, take time away from what we were all hired to do, which in my case is to teach the children math."

When Connie was finished, many teachers applauded. The principal looked embarrassed and the school nurse was frustrated. The discussion continued for quite some time, teachers were grumbling that they wanted to discuss the broken windows in the library and the problems with the bus schedule. The topic of the dental program was tabled for the time being, and the dentist informed the teachers that he would take the matter up at the next school board meeting.

Anyone who has insider knowledge of schools will recognize the above scenario. Played out in every community in the country is the tension between the academic program of the school and the "social improvement" programs that litter the school day and disrupt its flow.

How did it come to be that schools were responsible for the dental health of the young? When did we come to believe that the school day should be used to teach all manner of subjects beyond a core curriculum?

Contested Histories

In 1890 there were 224,526 school buildings in the United States, housing almost 13 million students in elementary school and 222,000 students in high school. Together these students accounted for 69 percent of the population aged 5 to 17. Over 77 percent of these students were in rural schools. Of 100 students in educational institutions at the time, 95 were in elementary school, 4 in secondary and 1 in postsecondary. Schools were age-graded. Instruction was in the form of recitation: students stood and recited their lessons. The majority of talk was teacher talk and the desks were bolted to the floor. At Steele High School in Ohio in 1896, the doors opened at 8:30 and closed at 1:00. The school day was divided into six periods, each 41 minutes long, with a 15-minute recess. There were four courses of study: classical, scientific, English, and commercial, each course of study lasting the full four years.[1]

Between the midnineteenth century and the midtwentieth century, the school year expanded from 12 to 36 weeks.[2] The length of the class periods has changed little, but otherwise schools have undergone a great deal of change. Perhaps the greatest change in the ways schools operate has been the broadening of the school's role. Today we firmly believe that schools can and should teach democratic participation and that school instruction should be based on child-centered pedagogical practices—both hallmarks of the progressive educational thought of the first part of the century. In addition, we collectively think that schools should be to some extent instrumental in changing society and should include intervention into the lives of children and their families. This conception of schooling was a central feature of progressive thought, born in part out of the historical reality of mass immigration in the early part of the twentieth century. Like immigration patterns of the mid-eighteenth century, this tide of immigration again put tremendous pressure on the schools to serve as institutions that Americanized newly arrived immigrants. In 1903, according to the journalist Adele Marie Shaw, "If it hopes to Americanize a school population chiefly of foreign parentage, [the school] must use abnormal means. . . . To educate the children of our adoption we must at the same time educate their families, and in a measure the public school must be to them family as well as school."[3]

The view of the schools as the instruments of Americanization has it roots in nineteenth-century battles over compulsory attendance laws. At that time, the vast majority of school truants were children of the foreign-born and it was with a fair degree of anti-immigrant sentiment that the battle for national attendance laws was waged by educators. "With concern about an undesirable class of immigrants on the rise, it was to the schools generally and to the social studies in particular that American leaders turned as the most efficacious way of introducing American institutions and inculcating American norms and values," writes the historian Herbert Kliebard.[4]

The "Americanization" movement in the early part of the century found common ground with leading educators of the day, who were convinced that the public school was the instrument best suited for molding American citizens. These educators believed that the "problem" of "making Americans" was complicated by the fact that if we "Americanized" children without Americanizing their parents we were creating an unbridgeable gulf between parents and children. Thus, by the mid-nineteen-twenties, schools were well on their way to building partnerships with parents in order to smooth the transition into life in the United States.

The belief that schools must create citizens can be considered part of the larger progressive agenda, which was that the schools can and should ameliorate social ills and soften social injustice. Indeed, many saw the schools as the place where American society could be cured of all its ills. This idea, central to the progressive movement, was captured in the short-lived journal *The Social Frontier,* which appeared from 1934 to 1943.[5] The first issue contained the following statement:

> Its [*The Social Frontier*'s] founding is definitely related to the new spirit of creative social inquiry which has been apparent among American educators and teachers during the past three or four years. If the hopes of its founders are to be realized, this new journal must become the expressive medium of

those members of the teaching profession who believe that education has an important, even strategic, role to play in the reconstruction of American society.[6]

Coupled with the believe that schools can and should contribute to changing society for the better was the child-centered philosophy embedded in progressive thought. Drawing on the writings of Rousseau and a child psychologist, Stanley Hall, progressives wanted schools and their programs to meet the needs of the individual child. Lawrence Cremin writes about the range of high school curricular topics inspired by new understandings of adolescent psychology:

> Were adolescents newly interested in vocational education? High School would offer industrial and agricultural education for young men and domestic science for young women. Were adolescents interested in "large living wholes?" High schools would offer comprehensive courses in social studies in place of the separate disciplines of history and political science. Were adolescents preoccupied with sex? High schools would offer courses in family living and sex education. Did the range of individual differences increase among adolescents? High schools would offer differentiated curricula and varying versions of particular courses. Was adolescence a time of ebullient energy, or excess, or idealization? High schools would develop programs of athletic competition and social service. Was adolescence a time of plasticity, of unclarity, of susceptibility to perversion? High schools would establish guidance centers to ensure that youngsters entered upon the right path.[7]

The idea that we could use the schools as a vehicle for social engineering—that schools needed to serve as an Americanization instrument for the newly arrived foreign population—and advances in the science of pedagogy led to major transformations in the structure and content of schooling in the United States in the early part of the twentieth century. School systems expanded. The curriculum was reorganized and broadened. There were extended opportunities for vocational and physical education and a wide range of extracurricular activities was introduced. A strong belief in the importance of child-centered education led schools to redesign their space, to remake school desks and classroom fixtures to fit small children's size. Educators were busy devising tests to sort and categorize students that allowed for differentiated curriculum offerings, where students of differing levels of ability were exposed to different content. Schools became the place where vaccinations, health exams, meals, and psychological counseling were available. The result? The classroom that we have today, where dental health programs compete with reading instruction for the limited hours in the school day.

While some progressives were busy redefining the function and structure of schooling, others were reworking the content. In the late nineteenth century the National Education Association (NEA) established a committee to review the high school curriculum. The Committee of Ten, composed primarily of college presidents, published its report in 1893. They called for a broadening of the high school curriculum beyond the classics, which included Greek, Latin, and mathematics. This reform document, the first national committee to recommend a national agenda for the schools, made a strong case for the importance of giving all students a liberal education and rigorous mental training. Before the report, this rigorous training was considered to be best accomplished through study of the classical languages. The report, however, argued that Latin and Greek were not the sole subjects that required a mental workout and called for teaching modern languages, history, and the sciences. The Committee of Ten made the case that secondary schools were not just for students going on to college, but constituted the appropriate site for preparing youth for the "duties of life."[8] Some schools around the country adopted the recommendations in the report and broadened the high school curriculum to include history, the sciences, literature, and modern languages. But in 1900, a full 50 percent of high school students still studied Latin.[9]

Again in 1918 the high school curriculum was the subject of yet another national study conducted by the NEA, which resulted in the publication of "Cardinal Principles of Secondary Education." This document called for the high school core curriculum to be radically redesigned to be far less academically substantial. The curriculum's objectives included the area of health, command of fundamental processes, worthy home membership, ethical character, citizenship and vocation, and worthy use of leisure.[10] In addition, the reform package called for extensive programming in guidance and counseling, heavily dependent on testing. The report in many ways codified what was already happening in the schools. Dividing students into tracks and offering them different courses of study was already a "salient fact of American public school life in 1918."[11] Social changes identified by the committee that demanded a response by the schools included the need for schools to respond to the mechanization of labor, the ethnic diversity of the high school population, and advances in education theory.[12]

The rapid industrialization in the United States during this period also helped to establish the parameters of the American classroom that we have today. The demands of industry meshed with the goals of schooling to create a loosely coupled system whereby captains of industry worked hand in hand with educational leaders to design a new educational system suited for the industrial age. At the time, the United States was on the move, the Industrial Revolution was demanding more and more workers for its factories, and a classical education was thought to be of little use to factory workers. The strength of this belief made its way into the very architecture and structure of the school itself. Schools were to become like factories. Time was organized by bells that told students when to move, when to eat, and when to leave. Vocational education became mainstream. The eighteenth-century "academy" had had a decidedly practical bent, but the expansion of vocational education in the first part of the twentieth-century was driven by the needs of industry, and was given scientific support by the burgeoning testing movement, which allowed educators to sort students into educational programs suited to their potential life destinies.

Schools that do too much have their roots in this long historical movement to broaden the mission of public schools. When teachers reflect on the erosion of time for academic instruction, they are really raising the question of whether the mission of public schools ought to include all that they currently do. In the comprehensive high school of today, students, parents, and counselors choose from a wide range of options. Counselors design a program believed to be best suited to the student's future plans. Sports, public interest initiatives like the drug awareness program DARE, lunch-time clubs, and AIDS education all compete for the six and a half hours students are in school. As more subjects were added to the high school curriculum—in effect, more program tracks for students with different potential futures—the school day became ever more cut up and chaotic, until we reach the present time, when even after two decades of school reform in the majority of schools in the United States, most teachers in unrestructured public schools still teach over 120 students in six 51-minute periods.[13]

Most would agree that using the schools to solve social problems is a legacy of the Progressive Era. For many educators, to abandon that belief is to undermine the very foundations of modern education. But even John Dewey, a philosophical pragmatist and an intellectual father of progressive education—would want us to look at the consequences of these beliefs. And today, the consequence of our ambitiously expanded view of the purpose of schools is a chaotic, fragmented school day that often forces students to do their real learning at home as homework. Many progressive educators today acknowledge that schools themselves are part of the social order that they trying to change.

Even as I write this, I hear the voices of my intellectual ancestors in my head. To question the role of schools in solving social problems and to ask whether a broadened curriculum is essential to the well-being of children is to question my own deeply held beliefs about the purpose and content of education. As a public school teacher, I always shifted my lesson plan if a national event called for a class discussion. I taught as if I had all the time in the world, so I spent time on activities and lessons whose value I saw as directly related to the life of the students and their future, rather than on the English textbook. But that was twenty years ago. Today students are under tremendous pressure to perform. A culture in which precious time is given over to test preparation and testing rob precious classroom hours. Admission to college has never been more competitive. In the face of the changed reality of schooling, nothing less than a re-visioning is called for, even though doing so represents an about-face for me.

I recently listened to the lament of a new teacher who had spent a good deal of her first year preparing her sixth- grade class for a week-long trip to the Dominican Republic. She had done all the right things: science curriculum tied to the trip; intense year-long Spanish classes; reading Dominican literature; establishing pen pals. Her class raised funds so students who couldn't afford to go would be able to. In the end, the new teacher lamented that the time and energy the project consumed—in working with parents and students, in organizing—overrode the benefit students got out of the experience.

Her story reminded me of my early teaching days when we took our students to Europe. After the two-week trip, I realized that the only benefit the students got from the trip was the social bonding that took place on the tour bus. My colleagues and I concluded that the kids would probably have gotten as much educationally if we had just driven them around the freeways of Los Angeles in a school bus for two weeks. In our rush to make schools into communities—to offer children every kind of educational or social or cultural experience— we take on projects like these that seem in the end to be more about the desires of parents and teachers than the learning needs of kids. In our rush to have pictures from the "class trip" in the school yearbook we are unwittingly diverting much needed time and attention from the main task at hand.

I believe we are at a new historical moment, where a set of social forces is opening up space for a new definition of the mission of schooling.

There are growing arguments for rethinking the set of ideas that has driven the development of schools in the century just past. According to Marc Tucker, a leading spokesperson for national standards and head of the National Center on Education and the Economy, "[A] return to insistence that everyone master a demanding common academic core; commitment to high academic standards for everyone, irrespective of occupational choice or personal background . . . would be extraordinary by themselves after such a long commitment to principles and practices so deeply at odds with them."[14]

Tucker is reminding us that our current appetite for educational standards—now in place in all fifty states—is a departure from past educational thinking. For the past century we have built our schools on the belief that we were doing kids a favor by providing them with a differentiated curriculum, designed to "meet their needs." The number of programs we offer our students makes our school environment look more like a shopping mall than a classroom. And most progressive educators today now know that this system has been used to track poor kids into programs that prepared them for a life of few choices.

Education standards are designed to make public the learning goals we have for students. If well designed, they can drive curriculum, instruction, and assessment. The first round of standards setting, begun in the eighties, focused on content and performance standards for students: What do students need to know and be able to do? Setting the standards, however, raised more questions than were answered: Who is accountable for higher levels of student learning? More specifically, what portion of responsibility for higher student learning must be borne by the schools, what portion by the community, what portion by the family, and what portion by the students themselves? During a recent TV interview, the commissioner of education in Maine, Duke Albanese, said that if we are going to meet the state's new learning goals, students must do more homework. A too-easy answer to a complex question, and not the full story. Most educators agree that if teachers cannot teach to these higher levels, students will not learn to higher levels. Students will not do well on standards-driven assessments if schools do not provide opportunities for students to learn the material. Educators have started to become more comfortable with the idea of standards-driven curriculum guidelines; now they are beginning to understand that content standards are only the starting point of restructuring a national system of education.

The standards movement in this country demands something of the schools that previous reforms have not. Establishing a set of standards means that states have made significant decisions about the end purposes of education. We no longer have the imprecise language about education having to meet student needs. We have defined learning goals in very particular areas. This is a fundamental shift in our way of thinking about education, from looking at inputs to looking at outcomes. Standards look at course work and define what the outcome, the end product, should be. In the past, when we wanted to improve student achievement we increased the number of courses students were required to take—increased the inputs. For example, in the early eighties there was a national push to improve science instruction in the schools, so most states added an additional required science class to the high school program, on the assumption that this would lead students to learn more science. Standards flip this conception on its head. We now have determined exactly what science we want students to learn at various points in the schooling and set standards at that point.

But the story does not end with defining and adopting education standards. In state and national organizations work is under way to design instruments to measure student achievement of learning standards. Educators know that next on the standards agenda is a focus on teaching and instruction, especially the demands a standards-based curriculum makes on instructional activities. According to Tucker and Codding, raising student achievement in this country will take nothing less than "a renewed moral commitment to our children and a willingness to set aside established ways of doing things in favor of a single-minded focus on results."[15]

Recent court action supports the view that a focus on results and the schools' responsibility to provide opportunities to learn is essential in the quest for raising student achievement. A 1995 decision by the New York Court of Appeals found that the state has the responsibility to provide the resources for students to achieve the state purposes in education.[16] In this case, having learning standards in place meant that the court could identify the state's purpose in education, a significant improvement over the past with no clear definition of the "state's purpose," when it came to matters educational.

Holding schools accountable for higher levels of student learning is now on the national education agenda, and standards can be a powerful force in helping communities refocus their resource allocations and energies to achieve that end. If they do not, we will be seeing more cases like the one in New York. Students will struggle to meet new learning standards and states will have to grapple with the level of responsibility of each stakeholder in the system for student failure. Criticism of standards has rightly focused on how student achievement of standards will be impacted by the extreme inequality of educational opportunity in this country. How can we fairly hold students to higher educational standards when they attend substandard schools? How can we hold all students accountable to the same standards when their schooling opportunities are so vastly different?

An additional worry is that standards will be used to develop a narrowly focused testing system like the high-stakes testing being done in some states. Many believe that when teachers teach to tests, individual student needs and strengths get eclipsed. When tests determine advancement to the next grade, schools must be able to prepare students well for the tests. Many districts have had to develop summer-school and after-school programs designed to help students meet higher standards. In Baltimore, for example, fully one third of the students spent the summer of 2000 in school. Providing opportunities for students to learn is recognized as an important responsibility of schools has been an important by-product of adopting education standards.

Supporters of national standards like Marc Tucker argue that they not only change the historical direction that schools have been moving, they actually provide for a more equitable education system. Regardless of one's political take on education standards, there can be little doubt that the standards movement will have a tremendous impact on what and how kids learn and how they are tested.

It is notable that though the standards movement has focused on curriculum, assessment, and instruction, the power of standards may ultimately lie in their ability to influence time and budget priorities in our schools. Having seen the costs of schools that do too much, we can use standards to recalibrate their educational mission. Let us turn next to how budgets are made, in order to see the possibilities for how they might—with a boost from standards—be changed.

CHAPTER 3

Counting Costs: The Trap of Incremental Budgeting

*H*ow we spend the school day is determined to a great extent on how we spend the school dollar. Money determines the quality, quantity, and nature of the school day. Like the tally of how time is spent in a typical day in school, an analysis of how school money is spent can reveal our values, priorities, and misguided ideas about schools and can point us in the direction of eliminating counterproductive expenditures.

In fact, such records actually exist in every community in the form of school budgets. However unglamorous they may seem, budgets are, I will argue, the place both where all of us as citizens can see most clearly what our communities' priorities are for schools and where we as citizens, teachers, and administrators can have the largest impact on shaping priorities—if we understand how. This chapter will be a primer on school budgets, and a call to arms. A later chapter will lay out what we all can do.

In the United States the school budget is a fiercely local phenomenon, one of the most important expressions of local democracy. The school budget, developed locally, determined by state and federal mandates and community traditions, and augmented by a complex formula of state aid, is the single largest item in any town budget. State and federal mandates for programming and testing may drive much of what schools offer, but more often than not, those mandates come unfunded. It's up to local communities to decide how to pay for the innovation. This usually involves trading off another budget line or raising property taxes to fund new school programs to comply with these mandates.

Although most aspects of schools have been debated over the past century—the content of schooling and the length of the school day and year, for example—the idea of the local control of schools is sacrosanct in the United States. Local control of schools is assured in part by the purse string, and local funding of schools in part ensures that schools will be locally controlled. The idea of local control of schools is a very American one and is, I will argue, a unique opportunity for our democratic engagement.

But the result is also one of the most complex and convoluted ways of funding schools in the world. Amazingly, a law passed over 350 years ago gives us the structure that we live with today.

"Ye Olde Deluder Satan"

In 1647, the General Court of Massachusetts enacted the "ye olde deluder Satan" law, which was designed to help people stay out of the hands of Satan by teaching them to read and write. The provision required every town of more than fifty households to hire a teacher of reading and writing and to provide for paying his wages. Towns of over one hundred households were required to have a grammar school to prepare the youth for possible entrance into the university. This law established that control and financing of education was a state, not a federal, responsibility. The Old Deluder Satan Act gave local governmental bodies the right to levy taxes for education. Other New England colonies followed suit. Outside of New England, colonies had private and parochial schools for children whose parents could afford the tuition and who could afford to forego the child's labor while he attended school.

By the eighteenth century, the arguments for the establishment of state-sponsored schools (though still largely funded locally) shifted from keeping Satan at bay to emphasizing the importance of education for building a democracy. Jefferson was perhaps the most vocal advocate of free, public education. In 1787 he wrote to James Madison saying, "Above all things, I hope that the education of the people will be attended to; convinced that on this good sense we may rely with the most security on the preservation of a due sense of liberty."[1]

According to the census in 1850, only about one half of the children in New England were provided with a free education. In other parts of the country, the portions of children receiving free education were much smaller, one sixth in the West and one seventh in the Middle states.[2] Arguments for the importance of free, public education in a democracy remained the rallying cry for those who sought to ensure the development of a national system of education. One of the more eloquent spokespersons of the movement for universal education was, Thaddeus Stevens, a legislator from Pennsylvania, who in 1835 stated:

> If an elective republic is to endure for any great length of time, every elector must have sufficient information, not only to accumulate wealth, and take care of his pecuniary concerns, but to direct wisely the legislatures, the ambassadors, and the executive of the nation—for some part of all these things, some agency in approving or disapproving of them, falls to every freeman. If then, the permanency of our government depends upon such knowledge, it is the duty of government to see that the means of information be diffused to every citizen. This is a sufficient answer to those who deem education a private and not a public duty—who argue that they are willing to educate their own children, but not their neighbor's children.[3]

A belief in the importance of education for sustaining a strong and vibrant democracy has been a central feature of the way in which Americans have come to understand their schools. We believe that education is a necessity for our way of governing. Progressive educators go one step further and argue that schools themselves must be democratic.[4] John Dewey taught that in order for citizens to value democracy they must have experienced it in schools. Since then, educators have debated issues such as how to instill democratic principles in the young, whether democracy must be experienced to be valued, and what the role of the schools is in ensuring democratic structures. Today, the strongest argument against vouchers and home schooling is that students and their families who select out of public schools fail to get the skills necessary to navigate the give-and-take of democratic life.

Money and Schools

In recent years the foundational principles underlying the purposes of education in this country have shifted. To many, education has come to be seen as an investment in human capital. Improved educational performance has been linked to workforce development since the publication of the influential report *A Nation at Risk*.[5]

Tying educational reform to economic productivity has been a double-edged sword for educators. On the one hand, it has arguably narrowed the focus of public discourse about the role of schools, pushing debates about the democratic role of education aside to some extent. It has certainly brought more economists into leadership and policy-setting roles in the field of education.

But at least linking education to economic development has put educational reform on the national agenda, a fact that we should all be glad of. In addition, it has brought more economists into the arena of educational analysis. Economists have applied the tools of their trade to schools, conducting input/output analysis, especially production-function studies, trying to uncover what makes a difference in improving schools.

This sort of analysis has led some to the conclusion that money has little bearing on the quality of education. The first and perhaps most famous production/function analysis of schooling was the Equal Educational Opportunity Report, unofficially called the Coleman report, which came out in 1966. Conducted by James Coleman for the federal government, the report shocked the nation by claiming that the influence of family background and quality of community on academic achievement was as great as if not greater than the schools' influence. Many concluded that the Coleman report gave us clear evidence that increased spending on education could do little to override the impact of poor communities, illiterate parents, and unmotivated youth. Economists have spent the last forty years debating whether money makes a difference in schools.

Experts disagree on this issue. Richard J. Murnane, an economist from Harvard, summarizes the current state of evidence about spending and schools with the conclusion: "In my view, it is simply indefensible to use the results of quantitative studies on the relationship between school resources and student achievement as a basis for concluding that additional funds cannot help public school districts."[6]

But this debate about whether bigger budgets make better schools is one I want to put aside in order to discuss a prior question: How do we make better schools with the money we have? Unless we know how to do that, we won't know how best to spend our school money, no matter how much we have at our disposal. And before making spending decisions, we first have to understand how budgets work.

Making and Selling the School Budget

When a small coastal community in California cut the high school budget by 7 percent, the high school principal did what most school administrators tend to do: he delegated. Calling the staff together, the principal began, "I have asked each department chairperson to work with their department to make a seven percent cut from each department's budget. I wanted to be fair in distributing the cuts equally and I know that each department will deal with these cuts differently.

"I feel confident that each department will make decisions that will represent the best thinking of each team. Remember, we must keep the education of our students in the forefront of our decision making, so look at your budgets with the students' academic needs in mind. The community will want to see increases in test scores next year and there is talk that your salary increase may be tied to increases in test scores."

Staff grumbling had been going on all day since the news of the cuts started circulating, and now it continued. Teachers asked why they had to play a zero/sum game with their peers. Some wondered whether there wasn't a more systematic approach to budget cutting, which had become commonplace in the state in the last few years. A taxpayer revolt in the early seventies had meant drastic cuts in school budgets in the state, with some districts losing as much as 30 percent of their budget over five years. During that time, the community, like others, had organized a nonprofit foundation, Save Our Schools (SOS), which had raised considerable money to cover some of the budget shortfalls. Yet SOS was much more interested in sponsoring the "frills" of education, so the cost of textbooks and of raising teacher salaries were rarely on the top of their giving lists. Still, the sports programs, school social events, and the like benefited from the community's largesse.

As the staff meeting struggled forward, the principal continued to make his plea for each department to take care of its share of the budget cuts. Some wondered whether the counseling office was taking a cut. A few asked whether the principal had discussed with the community the impact of these cuts, coming as they did after four years of similar cuts. Some implored him to look at all the school's programs and consider cutting whole programs rather than crippling every program. Others wondered whether there wasn't a way to factor in the contributions from SOS that certain programs received.

A courageous physics teacher stood up. "You have put us in a position where we have to fight with each other over money. Given that fact, I would like you to consider that over the last five years the science department has seen its operating budget shrink by 21 percent and its staff be cut by one faculty member and three teaching assistants. We have seen no such cuts in the athletic programs in this school. We still field six different teams each season, each team still has the same number of coaches, and the teams have all had new uniforms within the last four years. We all know that SOS has provided some of the funds for this, but those of us who teach in the core programs in this school must live with cuts while the athletic programs simply go to the community for money when they need it. The message this sends to us is that this community cares little about basic education and more about sideshows for the community. And you, sir, have not played a leadership role in this community by helping them to see how their values and choices are crippling the education of their children." As the physics teacher sat, a few teachers rose to applaud him.

The principal had known that this was coming. SOS giving had created tremendous tension among the faculty. And he didn't disagree with the physics teacher—in fact, the community did care more about a good show on the basketball court than it did that the beakers in the biology lab were few and far between. It wasn't his fault that uniforms for the marching band were a higher priority for the community than teacher assistants. Beyond the problems associated with the way SOS distributed funds to the school, he had to agree with the sentiment of the faculty that across-the-board cuts were, well, the easy way out. Long ago, he had arrived at the conclusion that the most ex-pedient and least politically volatile way to make the cuts was across the board. He knew that each school program had a vocal group of supporters whose wrath he and the community would suffer if he cut their beloved program. Last year when he cut an alternative program for at-risk students he had to hide in his office for weeks while the local paper ran endless stories about the ill treatment some students receive at the school and about the school's responsibility to educate all stu-dents. Former students of the alternative school and their parents sent letters to the editor, as did local business leaders who had worked with these students. In retrospect he determined that it would have been better to cut the program's budget in half and let it die a natural death than to make the decision to cut it entirely. He was not going to make that mistake a second time.

Scenes similar to the above have become commonplace in Ameri-can schools since the late seventies, which brought the advent of the "taxpayer" revolt. In California in 1978 voters passed Proposition 13, an amendment to the state constitution limiting local property tax rates and making it more difficult for local governments to increase those taxes. Proposition 13 forced cuts in state revenues by close to 25 percent, the vast majority of the hit being taken by local school dis-tricts. State appropriations from the state's general fund reduced the net loss to schools to around 11 percent in the first year, but neverthe-less the effects on the California's public education system, once the pride of the nation, were devastating. Across the nation, many other states followed suit with similar taxpayer relief plans, all of which have had the effect of forcing drastic cuts in school budgets around the country. These scenes of large budget cuts will soon be repeated around the country. Since school funding is tied to enrollment num-bers and the birth rate is dropping in the United States, many commu-nities will experience shrinking school budgets.

What are the key features and pitfalls of the budget-making pro-cess? How could it be different?

School Budgets 101

Although the legal authority over schools resides with the state, lo-cal communities assume the managerial and fiscal responsibility for

them. Controlled by a local school board, money for the school budget is set by a rather complicated funding mechanism that combines
local, state, and federal dollars. Today the majority of state governments contribute about 50 percent of the money needed by schools in
the state. Exceptions include on one extreme Hawaii, which funds
close to 100 percent of each school budget, and on the other New
Hampshire, which funds less that 10 percent. Within states, historically, wide disparities in communities' fiscal resources have existed in
all fifty states. The move toward state and federal contributions to local school budgets was designed, in part, to smooth out some of the
disparities and ensure at least rudimentary levels of education for all
of America's children, regardless to the economic level of their community. Now, however, many no longer see equalizing school funding
as a solution to the problems of underperforming schools in poor
communities. (The 2002 federal education bill gives parents in underperforming schools the right to move their children to better schools.
No doubt this represents a compromise position between those wanting a national voucher system and those wanting increased federal
funding for poor schools.)

The primary source of funds for schools is a town's revenue from
property taxes. The secondary source of funds comes from the state
through a variety of grants, programs, and a complicated funding
formula designed to determine what the state's contribution to local
funds will be. This formula has never been fully successful in equalizing funding across a state. In some states the discrepancy in school
spending between high-wealth and low-wealth districts is enormous.[7]
In many states, you can tell the wealth of a town by the percentage of
school funds that come from the state—the higher the percentage of
state funds, the lower the local property tax rate.

Schools calculate a "per-pupil cost," which refers to the amount of
money that the school needs to educate one student. These costs vary
widely across a state. In some states, one district might have a $5,600
per-pupil cost, while at a school across town, the cost might be as high
as $9,000.

The state revenue share for each per-pupil cost is actually based on
the enrollment figures from the year before. If a school has a sud-
den influx of students, there will be a funding gap. This is why schools

are so picky about absenteeism and so hard on parents about writing notes when students are absent. A teacher's attendance sheet is a legal document and is the basis for funding formulas.

How a school uses this money is the important aspect of school budgeting for us. Most school districts use a budget process called incremental budgeting. Each year, as revenues go up or down, administrators must be certain to cover fixed costs. These include material and staff and personnel costs, which in most districts account for between 70 and 85 percent of the school budget. In years when revenues increase substantially, new programs and new equipment purchases might be possible, but for the most part, budgets are set each year in an incremental fashion. There might be changes at the margins, but the categories and budget lines are set. This budgeting process, as we shall see, accounts in large part for the entrenched nature of the school program. The amount in a line-item of the budget effectively ensures the continuance of a program. As long as budgets are constructed by adding or subtracting a few dollars to each line item, substantial change is unlikely to occur.

Looking at a school budget can be an off-putting experience (see Figure 3.1 on pages 56–57). Schools are under local jurisdiction, and each school budget is constructed locally, so there is tremendous variation in the way budgets look, but a few signposts will help the first-time budget reader get oriented. Across the top of the budget there is almost always a number of columns for the current-year expenditures, the proposed budget for the coming year and the percentage of difference between the two. Sometimes there is a column that includes budget totals for the previous year and columns with budget projections out into two years. Line-item budget numbers can be twelve digits long. Budget categories are often abbreviated and seem designed to confuse— to keep the public out of the business of understanding what school programs actually cost. For example, my community uses "fund xfer: non-athletic" to mean funds used for extracurricular activities that are not part of the regular athletic program. Once your eyes get adjusted to the minuscule print on a budget document and you get beyond what may be an aversion to a page full of abbreviations and large numbers, the budget is pretty straightforward.

Most budgets start with the revenues that come into the school,

FIGURE 3.1 Bar Harbor School Department Revised Final Budget*

		2000–01 Actual Expend.	2001–02 Current Budget	2001–02 Anticipated Expend.	2002–03 Proposed Budget	$ Difference	% Difference	Explanation
Regular Instruction								
110–100–110	Teacher's Salaries	1195721.18	1228100	1253409	1333245	105145	8.56	Curr Staff w/o Rick+1/2 W.L+40%K.S.
110–100–111	Summer School	13833.8	12000	7000	8000	−4000	−33.33	
110–100–112	Ed. Tech. Salaries	42612.78	25000	35165	35580	10580	42.32	6 Ed. Techs minus Title I
110–100–113	Learning Labs	0	14000	0	8000	−6000	−42.86	
110–100–115	Literacy Specialist	0	2500	2500	2500	0	0.00	
110–100–120	Substitutes—Other	32583.81	28000	23000	15000	−13000	−46.43	
110–100–121	Substitutes—Prof. Dev.	0	0	0	13000	13000	#DIV/0!	
110–100–200	Soc. Sec./Medicare/Retire.	13159.42	16500	16500	18510	2010	12.18	
110–100–210	BC/BS: Tchrs./Ed. Techs.	238304.99	281639	296098	277400	−4239	−1.51	
110–100–260	Tuition Reimb.: Taxable	4091.65	2000	2000	3000	1000	50.00	
110–100–261	Tuition Reimb.: Non-Tax.	4997.85	7500	7500	6500	−1000	−13.33	
110–100–320	Prof. Svcs.: Counsel/ESL	7175.7	12000	10000	9000	−3000	−25.00	
110–100–433	Contr. Svcs.: Equip. Repair	3987.89	4000	4000	4000	0	0.00	
110–100–434	Science Kits		4500	4500	4500	0	0.00	
110–100–580	Staff Travel	778.85	1500	1500	1500	0	0.00	
110–100–610	Teaching Supplies	31993.84	33000	33000	28000	−5000	−15.15	
110–100–640	Textbooks	28935.7	20000	10000	12000	−8000	−40.00	
110–100–650	Computer Software	1991.92	4000	4000	2000	−2000	−50.00	
110–100–730	Replace/Purch of Equip.	10377.54	3000	3000	4000	1000	33.33	
110–100–810	"Dues, Fees, Conf."	4149.59	6000	6000	6000	0	0.00	
Total Regular Instruction		1634696.51	1705239	1719172	1791735	86496	5.07	
Total Special Education		409275.37	455993	431543	458337	2344	0.51	
Co-Curricular								
410–100–130	Salaries: Extra-Curricular	30058.59	31000	32000	36000	5000	16.13	

410–100–200	Soc. Sec./Medicare	982.01	1700	1400	1900	200	11.76
410–100–330	Fine Arts Performances	2196.51	4000	2000	3000	-1000	-25.00
410–100–430	"Contr. Svcs.: Officials, etc."	3900	4000	5000	5000	1000	25.00
410–100–610	Supplies	5315.98	2500	2500	2750	250	10.00
410–100–642	Periodicals	0	100	100	100	0	0.00
410–100–730	Replace/Purchase Equipment	3104.65	3000	3000	3000	0	0.00
410–100–810	Dues/Fees/Conferences	250	750	750	500	-250	-33.33
Total Co-Curricular		45807.74	47050	46750	52250	5200	11.05
Total Food Services		30000	32000	34000	37000	5000	15.63
Total Guidance		47342.21	55513	55230	59121	3608	6.50
Total Health Services		31574.09	35593	35107	37121	1528	4.29
Total Improve. Of Instruction		14585.93	22500	21500	21000	-1500	-6.67
Total Library & AV		62628.06	70925	70840	76547	5622	7.93
Total Technology		0	0	0	68624	68624	#DIV/0!
Total School Committee		8719.26	11960	18900	9960	-2000	-16.72
Total Office of Supt.		120352	129084	129084	167151	38067	29.49
Total Office of Principal		211371.91	231374	230467	239615	8241	3.56
Total Oper. & Maint.		313246.15	327698	319851	348662	20964	6.40
Total Transportation		127841.39	133900	133200	155500	21600	16.13
Total Capital Outlay		4020	3000	3000	3000	0	0.00
Total Insurance Svcs.		8273.84	11700	9500	12500	800	6.84
Contingency							
Grand Totals		3069734.46	3288529	3273144	3553123	264594	8.05

*A condensed summary of a small town's school budget, with a couple of major categories (regular instruction and co-curricular) broken out by budget line.

which usually are broken out into local, state, and federal and an assortment of other revenue sources: students who pay tuition from other districts to attend a school; the funds left over from the previous year; and perhaps revenues from school-sponsored events. This page contains a total amount of revenue that the school has for the coming year. The rest of the budget contains the school's expenditures; typical categories include regular instruction, special education, vocational training, cocurricular (those after-school-type activities like sports and drama), guidance and counseling, library, transportation, maintenance, administration, and capital outlay. Some states might have additional categories, but for the most part these general categories must be included.

Under the broad category of regular instruction you will usually find teacher salaries and benefits, textbooks, computer software, teaching supplies, equipment, and contracted services. In a high school budget, regular-instruction budget numbers typically are broken out by department. Numbers for other categories—insurance, transportation, library, and the like—are total-school numbers.

Under which category administrators put costs can vary widely from state to state, within a state, and even within a district. For example, sometimes professional development costs appear as a regular-instruction cost and sometimes in a different category like instructional improvement; computer costs can appear as its own separate category or be broken down under each department in a high school budget. The last page of the school budget will include a grand total that must match pretty closely the grand total from the revenue page. Generally it is the principal's job to get these two numbers to match.

In the ideal scenario, a principal must propose the constructed budget to the school board and the community. It is the school board's job to sell the budget to the town and it is the community's job to be certain that the school budget reflects the will of the community. Prior to the public budget meeting, school budget battles are waged in faculty meetings. Community members lobby principals on and off the golf course to increase funding for their special interests and custodial crews warn of boilers about to break. In addition, principals watch carefully for announcements of state and federal mandates for new programs that local districts will have to fund.

In reality, school administrators must serve two masters. The dual mission of the school system is to educate students and to make effective use of taxpayer funds. These contradictory missions force administrators to spend much of their time in elaborate budget machinations each year, as they try to reconcile the expense of education with the often stingy nature of local taxpayers. In the case of some large school districts, this work is done for the district as a whole; there is no school-by-school breakdown available for public discussion.

For the most part, budget construction consists of matching costs to expected revenues. And each year, administrators appeal to the community for funding increases. Heating systems break, new members to the community increase school enrollments, textbooks become out-of-date and new teaching practices demands new staffing patterns. Administrators must balance the educational needs of the children with a community's desire to hold the line on the school budget. This complicated budgeting process has led many administrators to see the school budget as a marketing problem: how to sell the school budget to the general public. Principals construct elaborate spreadsheets and PowerPoint presentations to show the impact on each taxpayer's pocketbook of a proposed budget increase. This form of budget selling lets taxpayers know the bottom line of school budget increases, but it does little to inform them about the cost of specific school programs and affords little opportunity for the community to come together and ask hard questions about specific school programs.

The public forum in which school budgeting occurs is the school board. Lay members of the community get elected to serve on school boards, which gives them control over hiring superintendents, structuring budgets, setting policy, and establishing priorities for the local system. Their meetings, always open to the public, are rarely attended by more than a reporter from the local paper and a few parents with pet projects to support. School board meetings could be the forum for a much more democratic way to run schools, something we will discuss in detail later. Typically, however, the school board is a structure that forestalls innovation and change.

When a few vocal community members get exercised by a topic, by sending as few as twelve people to a school board meeting they can successfully drive an initiative through the school board, forcing action by the administration. For example, a few members in a community might want soccer to be added to the athletic offerings of the high school. These community members can lobby their school board members, bring a proposal to the board, and get interested parents to attend the meeting and speak in support of the proposal. The discussion rarely includes the related discussion of what athletic program should be removed to make way for a new one. The structure is such that it ensures that vocal parents have access to policy makers, but it does not ensure that a wider public discussion about the true costs of the adding another program will follow. Incremental budgeting practices send the principal back to the office to shave a few dollars from here and there to free up resources for the new program that a few community members demanded.

School board members are elected officials and must run for office in their local communities. Sadly, in many communities, seats on the school board remain vacant for up to a year before the community can find someone willing to sit on the board. Often parents run for the board because they have an agenda to settle with a particular school. For example, recently, opponents of whole-language instruction, a method for teaching reading in the elementary school, have worked to elect school board members whose sole intent has been to overturn whole-language instruction in a school. It is not uncommon for business groups to ensure that they have representation on the local school board. I remember one meeting of a local real estate association where they spent an hour electing someone who would then run for the school board. They were very focused on making sure that their interests—the need to keep property taxes low—should be voiced on the school board. Elected members of watchdog groups often compete with interested citizens wishing to serve on the school board. The good news is that often members who start out being committed to their constituency soon find themselves having to balance their constituents' demands against those of the larger school community.

The bad news is that decision making based on solid educational research is not the modus operandi for local school boards. The vast amount of information boards must act on, the legal requirements related to in education, and changes in approaches to teaching and learning all mean that lay board members must deal with an enormous amount of complicated material. Districts do not devote time or money to training school board members, so communities must rely on school administrators to make solid recommendations to the board. This is not a recipe for innovation and fresh thinking about education. Those of us who have spent our lives at school board meetings know that the most common reason board members give for voting the way that they did on a particular issue is "This is the way we did it when I was in school."

The Search for "Payoff": Looking for Ways to Save Money

The tax revolt of the seventies and eighties led to an avalanche of writing on how to hold down school costs. Administrators who have saved their districts money are local heroes. Cost-saving strategies typically include cutting administrative services and containing costs in noninstructional areas. Administrators renegotiate contracts with providers, search for cheaper transportation companies, and buy better equipment so the maintenance staff can become more efficient. Tactics to shave $15,000 here and $50,000 dollars there abound. Principles for cutting costs without compromising quality are published in professional journals. Education scholars argue that without a radical restructuring in how we spend our educational dollars, we will never meet national goals of higher student achievement. For the most part, however, these recommendations never challenge the incremental budgeting process used by schools.

Policy analysts and scholars have been studying school spending patterns across the country in order to inform the public debate about the relation of academic achievement to the ways schools spend their dollars. Most notably, the Finance Center for the Consortium for Policy Research in Education (CPRE) has been conducting extensive studies on how the school dollar gets spent in all 50 states. Although they found that funds have been distributed unfairly and used ineffectively, they conclude that although funds have not been squandered, they been not been used wisely. Their conclusions: no smoking guns and no academy awards.[8] They present interesting insights into where education money comes from and the ways the school dollar gets spent.

Studies from CPRE show that over the 35 years between 1960 and

1995, the federal and state contribution to education increased as the local contribution decreased. Spending on education has increased nationally by close to 207 percent in this time period—and the spending disparities have also increased.[9] Some children in the country have $2,500 spent on them by their public school, while others are allocated $15,000. Teachers made more money in 1990 than they did in 1960, but they have not gained much ground compared to other workers with similar levels of education.

Only 40 percent of the school dollar goes to fund indirect instructional costs like maintenance, transportation, administration, and professional development, although it is hard to get accurate figures here. Districts differ in how they report indirect expenditures; for example, professional-development costs are listed by some districts as administrative costs and others as direct instructional costs. High- and low-spending districts alike report a 60 percent budget expenditure on the instructional program. Not only is this figure constant across districts, but also researchers found that staffing for core academic subjects varies little by spending levels.

Even though one district may spend thousands of dollars more per pupil than another, staffing in core academic subjects was exactly the same. These staffing patterns mean that significantly less than 50 percent of the school budget is spent on teachers in core academic areas. Researchers refer to these as the "fiscal regularities" of education; districts spend the education dollar in remarkably similar patterns. They conclude that since the public has a substantial investment in education, the system needs to be restructured so that it "pays off" in terms of increases in student achievement over the next ten years.

Scholars at the Finance Center of CPRE acknowledge that understanding how education dollars get spent is the first step in a process that must include learning how those resources affect student learning. The next step, Lawrence O. Picus and James L. Wattenbarger argue in *Where Does the Money Go?*, must be to direct resources to those activities that have a powerful impact on student performance:

> As we attempt to understand the impact of educational resources on student outcomes, gaining a stronger knowledge of how existing resources are used by school districts is important. The [CPRE] study conducted under the "What Money Buys" banner have provided a great deal of new data on how

resources are allocated. The next step is to learn how those resources affect student outcome, and to find ways to direct future educational resources toward methods that improve student performance.[10]

Like the findings of the National Education Commission on Time and Learning, CPRE's work calls on us to align budget allocations with mechanisms to increase student learning. Together, these two major reports provide us with the necessary ammunition to call for a major restructuring of how school dollars are spent in our communities.

Potholes in the Road to Financial Restructuring

There are obstacles to be overcome if we are to significantly restructure the school budget. If we want to move beyond selling a school budget to a leery community and into the business of directing educational resources toward increased student achievement, a number of current practices will have to be changed. I offer the following prime suspects in the line-up.

The full-plate syndrome: Schools are famous for adding new programs without eliminating existing ones. Teachers call this the "full-plate syndrome," lamenting that we keep adding things to the plate but never taking anything away. Most of us can understand this best by looking at the technology programs in schools. We would all agree that students need to become technologically fluent and most assume that schools are the places where that should happen. For the past ten years schools have scrambled to add computer classes to the schedule, build computer labs in the schools, and retrain teachers to teach using technology. But what did we take out of the school day or the teacher's training program as we added technology teaching and training? Nothing. We just added technology to the already overburdened school day. For the most part, schools have had to pick up the tab for this innovation, in terms of both time and dollars. While many districts have received grants, gifts, and federal money to build technology programs, few included the three-to-five-year replacement costs into their budgets or the massive costs of maintenance and upgrade as technology changes at lightning speed. The result: schools in poor communities have outdated computers in their computer labs. These computers cannot run contemporary software, do not prepare students to enter the technological age, and leave teachers bitter about the expense that they represent. Students in wealthy communities have computers at home that far outpace the computers in the schools, so the school computers are of little use to these students, who often have much greater skill levels and abilities than their teachers when it comes to using computers.

Next in the lineup: incremental budgeting. In this budgeting process budget categories are held constant while money is shifted around. Incremental budgeting is the handmaiden of the full-plate syndrome, and is a mechanism that keeps schools from changing. The budget-cuts scenario presented above is a very good example of the problem of using an incremental budgeting process, the type of process used almost exclusively in this country to determine the yearly school budget. By holding budget categories constant, school leaders avoid asking hard questions and abdicate the responsibility of looking to see if those categories make sense in today's world or in their communities. How does incremental budgeting trap schools into outdated programs and activities? Rather then examining each budget category on a regular basis, administrators adjust figures to meet projected budget shortfalls or windfalls. Competing self-interest on the part of departments and programs means that a zero/sum game pits teacher against teacher.

The need for accurate, clear, and concise information about the school budget has never been greater. According to James Guthrie, a leading policy analyst and expert on school finance, the problem of the lack of clarity in the school budget is significant: "In effect, the inability to determine precisely what is spent at a school prevents American education from being efficient, fair, or just. Few seemingly simple matters have such far-reaching consequences. More accurate spending information is an unusually small reform step possessing the potential for huge policy and practical rewards."[11]

The very categories that districts and schools use to construct their budgets do little to clarify how the school dollar gets spent. Take, for example, a budget published by the National Center for Education Statistics that shows expenditure allocations for different functions in 1991–92 for all the schools in the country. From categories itemized in the report, we see that expenditures for instruction are about 60 percent of the total budget. But what else do we know? Not much. Do we know what is included in budget categories listed by the report such as "Other," "Other Current," and even "Students"?

Given the governance structure of public schools and the role the general public plays in making decisions about school funding, nothing less than a public education campaign is needed.

An Alternative Direction

Conventional budget practices lock school programs in place in a very real and concrete way because they allocate money. Time becomes money in schools because what we devote resources to in the budget is what becomes the school program. And the programs we devote resources to are set in place by line items in the budget. No one remembers who originally decided on those categories or line items, but most administrators will tell you that they are set in stone. We don't question the category of a budget line; we merely question whether we should allocate $19,000 or $24,000 to that line item.

If we refocus the debate about budgets on educational aims and outcomes, as I argue we should, building into the budgeting process in a very concrete way the idea of schools' being held accountable to higher standards, new kinds of questions can emerge: Does it make sense that less than 50 percent of the teaching staff are teachers in core academic areas? Is it okay that only 60 percent of schools' resources are spent on direct instruction? Do we care that we don't really know how that other 40 percent is spent?

As James Guthrie reminds us, the first step must be to understand how the educational dollar gets spent today. And getting reliable information on this will be no small feat. We then need to look at the activities in the school day and determine whether they contribute to learning in core academic areas identified as education standards in each state. In chapter 5, we will explore a budgeting process called zero-based budgeting, designed to help communities look at and amend budget categories and allocations. Developed for California schools in the early 1970s, zero-based budgeting provides communities with the structure they need to engage all stakeholders in a school budget making process capable of radically shifting priorities. Chapter 5 outlines a process for communities to move themselves toward restructuring their resources so that they are in alignment with education standards. We have all the pieces in place to do the work of aligning resources so that they are used to achieve desired educational outcomes. The only question is: Do we have the will?

We have established education standards for our students in all states. They call for an increase in levels of academic achievement and set higher goals for the system as a whole. Doesn't it make sense that we would have to take apart the budget and look at each category to see how well it supports the goal of increasing academic achievement and meeting state education standards? Should we ask how activities in the school day contribute to meeting standards? A good place to start this analysis is with a part of the school program that consumes the resources of time and money but that is not listed as a learning outcome for any state in the nation—the interscholastic sports program.

CHAPTER 4

The Sporting Life in Schools

*W*hen educator Judy Codding arrived at her new job as principal at Pasadena High School, she was "astonished to discover the role that interscholastic sports play in the life of high schools in California."[1] Like most high schools, Pasadena High always had coaches and athletes assigned during the last period of the day either to PE class reserved for the athletes or to a coaching preparation session. Teacher-coaches themselves got the period before the last period of the day off to prepare for coaching. Codding found that this meant, for example, that an English teacher who is also a coach would finish with his or her teaching duties before lunch each day. This effectively eliminated any opportunities for teacher-coaches to meet with children outside the classroom, since all their available morning time was spent teaching classes.[2]

The master schedule in Pasadena had to be redesigned each semester when the sports activities changed. In a common practice, teachers had their teaching responsibility changed for a semester in which they had coaching duties. It was not uncommon for students to have different teachers each term in their yearlong classes like English, calculus, and a foreign language.

Pasadena High, a school of 2,200 students, in the late 1980s spent between $300,000 and $500,000 on its athletic program, seven times its textbook budget. As Codding notes, "A typical large high school in California might have fifteen sports teams, most of which have both girls' and boys' teams with freshman, junior varsity and varsity squads. Many have multiple coaches. At Pasadena High, we had eight to ten coaches for the eighty to one hundred kids on the football team. Wouldn't it be great if we had teacher-pupil ratios like that in the classroom?"

In a brave move, Codding took on the institutions of sport in her school because she saw something more important that needed doing:

> When I arrived at Pasadena, I was appalled at the low achievement of the students. If achievement was going to improve, we would have to give it the highest priority because there were no additional resources available. The most precious resources we could re-deploy were time—of both teachers and students—and money, especially the money spent on the faculty, which is the single biggest expenditure item in the schools. Something had to give, and that something, as I saw it, was the primary claim that the interscholastic sports program had on the time, budget and personnel of Pasadena High School.[3]

The competitive athletic programs that now drive many school schedules and budgets is a paradigmatic example of misplaced priorities— perhaps the most important example of how our schools try to do too much, to the detriment of learning. I will argue that athletics should be administered by organizations and institutions other than our public schools. This is not to say that community sports programs should not use the school facilities. My contention is that the funding, organizational support, and structure for competitive sports programs for young people should be provided by community organizations other than the public schools. The benefits for school budgets and school schedules could be enormous.

The Birth and Growth of School-Sponsored Sports

In the nineteenth century, sports were very much part of the street life of children. Urban student athletic associations and leagues were organized by the players themselves, raising money and sponsoring tournaments. By the turn of the century, the growing population of immigrants and their offspring were making some Americans suspicious of outsiders. In part driven by the anti-immigrant sentiment of the day, officials began to express concern about the rowdiness of sports teams. Already under way was the "Americanization" movement, which fostered the belief that newly arrived immigrants needed to become "Americans" and that schools were the best place where that training could be had. Believing that sports would be a great way to teach the American virtues of hard work, fair play, and competition, civic and school officials began calling for sports clubs to be housed in public schools. A public campaign was launched denouncing student-led leagues as unsafe. The movement allowed school administrators to place sports under the supervision of high school principals—and this was the birth of the institution of school sports.[4]

In their famous study undertaken in the 1920s, *Middletown: A Study in Modern American Culture*, Robert Lynd and Helen Merrell Lynd set out to conduct "a functional study of the contemporary life of this specific American community in light of the trends of changing behavior observable in it during the last thirty-five years."[5] Carefully choosing what they believed to be a city that represented contemporary American life and was also compact and homogeneous enough to be manageable in a study, with their study, begun in 1920 and repeated in 1935, they put Muncie, Indiana, on the map. *Middletown* gives us a solid picture of high school life in the early twenties.[6] Not surprisingly, high school looked pretty much then as it does now. The social life of the school is what captured the attention of the Lynds, who were particularly struck by the emphasis on sports:

> There were no high school teams in 1890. Today, during the height of the basketball season when all the cities and towns of the state are fighting for the state championship amidst the delirious backing of the rival citizens, the dominance of this sport is as all pervasive as football in a college like Dartmouth or Princeton the week of the big game. At other times dances, dramatics, and other interests may bulk larger, but it is the "Bearcats," particularly the basket-ball team, that dominate the life of the school.[7]

But it wasn't only the daily life of school during basketball season that led the Lynds to the conclusions they reached about the role of athletics in schools. The Lynds compared the 1894 yearbook with the 1924 yearbook. In 1894 athletics accounted for 5 percent of the pages;

by 1924 it was 19 percent.[8] When the Lynds returned to Middletown in 1935 for a follow-up study, they found that there had been an expansion in extracurricular activities. They also found that in 1931, at the height of the Depression, the town found enough money to give the high school basketball team gold watches when they won the state championship. The number of athletic teams had increased to include golf, tennis, wrestling, cross-country, volleyball, softball, and even horseshoes.[9]

By way of comparison, I checked my son's yearbook for 2001. Over 30 percent of the pages were devoted to athletic activities.[10]

According to the Lynds, community life at midcentury centered on basketball games on Friday night. Today there may be more activities competing for our time on Friday nights, but by all accounts school sports is still king. Pick up any small-town newspaper and see what school programs capture the largest share of the pages.

The most extreme form of the school as a palace to sports heroes is rendered powerfully in *Friday Night Lights: A Town, a Team, and a Dream,* by H. G. Bissinger, a journalist who followed the Permian High School football team from Odessa, Texas, through a season. The year is 1987 and the dream is the chance to win the state championship. Bissinger portrays a town whose only glory is football, past and present, and whose school is driven by one priority, sports. If you think this is an overstatement, consider the following. "The cost for boys' medical supplies at Permian was $6,750, the cost for teaching material for the English department was $5,040. . . . During the 1988 season, roughly $70,000 was spent for chartered jets."[11] Texas is known for its sports frenzy and in 1983 when the state began its school reform initiative, sports came under tough scrutiny.

The Case against Sports in Schools

School-sponsored sports, especially in our high schools—as the Pasadena story illustrates and the analysis below will show—serve a small number of students, distract from valuable teacher time, and waste money and time that could be better spent on other resources more relevant to teaching, the central mission of schools. Eliminating school-sponsored sports from our educational system would be one of the most powerful ways we have for addressing misplaced priorities in schools.

This does not mean that I am against sports. Competitive athletics builds important social skills in kids, it teaches teamwork and discipline. Sports programs keep many kids away from drugs and alcohol, at least during the season of the sport they are playing. Most school-age children need more physical activity, not less. Building a set of skills and a love for some form of physical exercise is now considered essential for life-long health. I am sure that if I had not been involved with competitive swimming in college, I would not find it as easy as I do to head for the Y at 5:30 A.M.. in the middle of the winter to swim. Despite these recognized benefits of sports, my point is that schools are not the place for institutionalizing sports. Competitive athletics can and should be housed in community organizations and businesses, leaving the schools free to concentrate on the teaching and learning needed if all students are to reach agreed-upon standards of academic attainment.

One caution: There are a number of roadblocks to any kind of meaningful discussion about the role of sports in schools. Perhaps the principal one is that the cost of the school sports program is very unclear. Questioning the role of sports in schools is often seen an un-American, and as a result, questioning the cost of sports programs often unleashes a contentious debate in communities. Getting accurate figures on the costs of sports programs and moving beyond the rancor will be essential if we are to get serious about our children's learning.

Computing the Costs

Calculating the time costs of sports programs in schools, especially at the high school level, is complicated: the culture of sports in many schools means that there is time off for pep rallies, away games, homecoming week, and the like and these consume a good part of the school year. Time lost to extracurricular activities is a universal complaint of educators, but researchers have yet to accurately quantify the time spent in sports-related activities.

Calculating the money costs of sports programs is even more difficult.[12] The costs of sports programs are embedded in a number of different budget lines, with the specific costs of the competitive athletic program undifferentiated from the total budget line. For example, in most school districts the costs of the transportation for athletic events is rolled into the total transportation costs for the district. Most school budgets have transportation costs as a budget item broken down into a variety of functional line items such as salary of drivers, maintenance, insurance, and fuel. There is typically not a line item for specific activities, such as transportation to athletic events. Similarly, the insurance costs for sports teams is part of a total insurance bill that a school district pays. When I asked my local high school for the cost of insurance for the football team, I was told that they didn't have the insurance costs broken down that far. The cost of maintaining a gym capable of hosting league gyms never appears as a line item in the school budget, but is usually part of the "operating and maintenance" category of the budget, and the specific costs for the gym are not broken out. The cost of maintaining a football stadium and field are never separated out of the school budget but also appear under the operations and maintenance section.

In the budget table that we looked it in chapter 3, interscholastic sports is not even a category. Most budgets typically identify some sports costs in a budget line labeled something like "co-curricular." The amount listed typically includes the cost of coaches, including benefits, conference fees, equipment, referees, and sometimes the salary of the athletic director. Included in the co-curricular budget is also the cost of other co-curricular offerings like music and drama. In small school districts, the athletic director is also the administrative head of all co-curricular offerings.

Supporters of athletic programs talk about the money that sports bring in, pointing to the revenues generated by gate receipts from games. Typically that amount can be found in the revenue section of a school budget under "sports events revenue." They rarely amount to a significant percentage of costs. For example, in my local high school, "sports events revenue" is $16,000. The identified, listed costs for the athletic programs are in the co-curricular budget section and total about 5 percent of a $5 million budget, or $250,000. These costs includes salaries and benefits for coaches, conference fees, supplies, and contracted services for referees, doctors, and other services specific to a sports program.

But even these figures are hardly accurate, since all co-curricular activities are lumped together, so the stipends for coaches are in the same budget figure as the stipends for the piano player who accompanies during school plays. Trying to get an accurate picture of the true costs of the athletic program, I worked with a local school board member analyzing the budget. By his calculations, when you include transportation, maintenance, insurance, and operations costs, the total cost of competitive athletics in my district is closer to 10 percent of the total school budget, or $500,000.[13]

So we see that the full costs of the competitive athletic program are not publicly disclosed, can be fully analyzed only with great effort, and as a result, are rarely publicly questioned. Even the Finance Center of the Consortium for Policy Research in Education (CPRE), which has conducted the most comprehensive analysis of the education dollar, did not break out the costs of the athletic programs in high schools![14]

One argument made for school sports is that many students participate. School sports supporters argue that with such widespread participation, sports deserves the limelight it gets. However, almost as difficult as calculating the actual costs of competitive sports programs is figure out the actual number of students served by these programs. Most students involved in high school sports compete in more than one. When I asked my local school administrator how many kids participated in sports, he proudly talked about the many kids who play sports. School administrators felt that whatever the cost, it was a small price to pay for the numbers of kids served by sports programs. I was told that out of the 450 kids in the school and well over 300 kids were enrolled in the sports program. But when I looked at the list of participants, the same 80 to 100 students showed up on the team lists. So what looked like 300 students enrolled in sports was actually about 95 students enrolled in three sports each. Other communities might have a broader range of students participating in sports, but not by much. I invite you to conduct the same survey at your local high school.

In addition to these problems associated with getting accurate data and costs on the athletic program, the very structure of the school system has contributed to the unquestioned acceptance of competitive athletics within the public school. The lack of career ladders in education is commonly known: there are few ways that teachers can "move up" professionally and few places for them to move into. But one sure route to the principalship of a school is through the sports program. A common career path in schools, especially at the high school level, is from PE teacher/coach to athletic director to principal. This pattern is perhaps less common now that women are entering school administration in greater numbers, but women administrators are still far more common at the elementary than at the high school level. Certainly school schedules, now appearing to be "fixed" features of the school day, were deliberately designed at a time when most administrators were fiercely interested in "their" teams, the ones many of them had recently coached before their promotions.

In most European countries, sports reside outside the public school system. Sports programs are part of elaborate club systems that operate at the community level. In some places sports are sponsored activities of the government.[15] In the United States, by contrast, sports have become a central component of public school life. This salient feature of sports in the United States has tremendous implications for the role of sports in American culture, for the relationship of sports to learning, and for the ways our education dollars are spent.

Recent research reports issued by the Brown Center on Education Policy of the Brookings Institution give us an interesting view into the life of high school students in this country and abroad. Researchers interviewed hundreds of foreign exchange students studying in United States high schools. These students reported that success in sports is much more important in the United States than in their own high schools. They don't believe American students work as hard as students from their home countries. The Brown report finds that changing this culture of sports in the high schools is central to increasing academic achievement in this country.[16]

Redefining the Role of Sports

For the most part, schools are still trying to offer the sports programs they have been offering for the past fifty years, but now they are also holding students to higher academic standards. Students—and schools—can't do everything. Something needs to give.

What would happen if we held all school programs to the same criterion: they must contribute to learning in core academic areas as defined by the state learning standards? One result might be that many activities now deemed central to the school mission would have to be housed somewhere else in the community. Could it be that high school athletic programs are the place to start when we ask the community to relieve the schools of unnecessary activities? Ross Perot thought so.

In 1983, Ross Perot was named to head the Texas Select Committee on Public Education, known as SCOPE, charged by the Texas legislature to "study the issues and continuing concerns relating to public education in Texas" ("Select Committee on Public Education, Recommendations," p. 3). The Perot Committee spent a year studying schools in the state and hearing from national education experts. Perot engaged in a media campaign to publicize the group's findings, centered in part on his strong critique of high school sports. He claimed that no reform in Texas schools was possible unless the sports culture was diminished. His very public critique, as summarized by a journalist, included railing against "Astroturf stadiums, electric cleat cleaners, towel warmers and 12-coach football teams as symbols of misplaced priorities. . . . [H]e wondered aloud why 600 of the state's 1,071 school systems spent all their local revenues on extracurricular activities." The majority of the reforms that SCOPE proposed passed through the legislature in 1984. Extracurricular activities were banished from the school day, and a highly controversial "no-pass/no-play" regulation whereby low-performing students were excluded from extracurricular activities became law.[17]

The Perot Committee's criticism of school athletics made headlines in Texas newspapers. Though the culture of school sports is still virtually intact in Texas, in many ways the Perot Committee's recommendations marked the beginning of state legislatures' entry into the regulation of high school athletics. Increasing numbers of states are imposing a no-pass/no-play policy. State legislatures have called for independent investigations of interscholastic sports programs and associations and have stripped power from state associations designed to regulate sports. Most state-level athletic association members are principals, coaches, and athletic directors. This narrow band of interests among the membership has led to the increased tension between state legislatures and state athletic associations.[18] At stake is control over how sports programs in this country will be conducted. The Perot Committee shined the spotlight on high school sports and found that the tail was wagging the dog. Increased sports-related regulation coming from state capitals should alert all of us to the need to scrutinize sports programs in our own communities.

We need to continue this work as citizens, school board members, parents, and teachers. The next step is changing the entrenched nature of sports in schools from the bottom up. Local communities need to subject spending on sports to scrutiny, and to begin the process of local political change that allows for the resources now spent on sports to be redirected to the core mission of schooling.

The Physical Education Continuum

It is important to remember that competitive after-school sports programs are not the only school programs that support the development of physical fitness. Schools have physical education programs to meet education standards in health and physical fitness, and all students must participate in these programs. This would not be changed if communities took responsibility for competitive sports and housed them outside the public school system.

No one can deny the immense importance of physical fitness in the development of a child and the maintenance of life-long health. Physical fitness, learned young, has powerful personal and social benefits. Enhanced physical fitness is known to increase quality of life, lower national health costs, and increase worker productivity.

In 1956, President Dwight D. Eisenhower established the President's Council on Youth Fitness, after research findings were released that showed American youngsters scored lower than their European counterparts on a battery of physical fitness tests. In 1960, President Kennedy changed the entity's name to the President's Council on Physical Fitness. President Johnson established the Presidential Sports Award program in 1972. Periodically throughout the last thirty years, presidents have kicked off national campaigns to increase student health through national physical fitness programs. In fact, recently President George W. Bush announced his own commitment to improving the health of the nation's young people. Health standards are a common feature of most states' education standards.

Beyond the health benefit of physical education are the values associated with team sports. Cooperation, competition, a sense of fair play, and the ability to follow rules are all important lessons for life that can be learned on the sports field. There are many ways that the values associated with sports can be built during a child's education. The free playtime of recess and physical education classes all provide opportunities for the development of important social and personal skills and for building physical abilities.

In elementary school, informal physical education takes place during the unstructured free play periods before school and during recess. Yet cutting out recess time, along with increasing homework assignments, has been the most popular step taken to meet higher academic standards. Across the country, school districts are getting more "time on task" by shortening the time for after-lunch recess and by cutting out altogether morning and afternoon recess. The loss of this unstructured playtime has been the subject of increasing debate among parents, and there has been much in the news about the move toward eliminating recess. There is as yet no systematic count of how many school districts are cutting recesses, but parent and teacher complaints nationwide are on the increase. School districts including Atlanta, Chicago, and Detroit are making recess optional or eliminating it altogether. In fact, in Atlanta they have built a few elementary schools without any playgrounds! In Virginia, the fear of losing recess has led the state to include "daily recess" in its accreditation standards. Researchers who have tackled to topic of recess have important findings for parents and teachers to contemplate.

Educators have known for decades that play and cognitive and social development are associated. For example, in the nineteen thirties Lev Vygotsky, a learning theorist, found that a key component of play is that it gives children an opportunity to act beyond their age: "Play creates a zone of proximal development in the child. In play, the child always behaves beyond his actual age, above his daily behavior: in play, it is as though he were a head taller than himself. As in the focus of a magnifying glass, play contains all developmental tendencies in a condensed form and is itself a major source of development."[19]

Vygotsky's work has led educators in this country to understand the importance of free play for cognitive development. For many students, recess is the only free time they had in the day. The plight of overscheduled children is becoming a more common lament in this country, and cutting recess time in schools contributes to children's loss of playtime. The long-term effect may be to slow development. In addition, the growing obesity among youngsters in the United States might well be caused in part by the elimination of recess.

Advocates of recess cite the importance of play to the development of social skills and cognitive abilities. An organization devoted to a child's right to play, the International Play Association, provides parents with research findings and resources to combat the anti-recess movement.[20]

Beyond the physical activity that students engage in during recess, physical education classes provide another opportunity during the school day for students to build the important social, physical, and emotional skills associated with sports. In schools, the co-curricular budget (which covers the after-school athletic programs) and the budget of physical education classes are two different categories. The physical education program, which all students are required to participate in, captures a much smaller amount of the identifiable sports budget of any school. Physical education costs come out of the instruction budget categories of most high school budgets. In the 2001 budget of my local school the physical education budget, not counting the salary and benefits of the teachers, was a mere $3,650. By way of comparison, the language arts budget totaled $17,550.

Physical education classes must be part of any well-rounded education program. Like recess activities, PE classes help students take a break from mental work, reduce stress levels in students, and help students burn off excess energy. Students need vigorous physical exercise because for the most part, they sit in desks for seven hours. As schools limit recess time at the elementary level in response to increased pressure for higher academic achievement and as high schools put their attention on athletic programs, physical education programs for all students are shortchanged and side-lined. For many elementary students in this country, PE happens just once a week. Recent findings of the rapidly rising obesity levels among the young in this country should give us all pause when we hear of yet another school limiting PE and cutting recess. Ironically, physical movement has been shown to increase academic achievement by increasing blood flow to the brain. In addition, rigorous physical activity helps potentially hyperactive students blow off steam.

All schools must have strong physical education programs, ones that help *all* students to meet education standards in physical fitness and health. Beyond that, do competitive sports have a role in the public schools? Or should community organizations take over the responsibility of running competitive sports programs? Imagine if a bank sponsored the women's basketball team, bank staff interested and prepared to coach basketball could work with the young women athletes, team practices could be held before work. The bank could perform meaningful community service by arranging employee schedules to meet the demands of coaching. The local police department might have an interest in taking on the football team. With this kind of authentic interaction between the police and the young people in the community, the police would not need to run programs in the local schools trying to improve the students' attitude toward them. Interested parents and community members would have opportunities to work with young people in ways not currently available to them, thus building intergenerational bonds that we all know are vitally important to youth development. The point is that looking to communities to sponsor competitive athletics frees the schools to do what they are charged with accomplishing and strengthens communities by calling on them to perform necessary work in the rearing of the children. It is hard to imagine that sponsoring a football program would have as overpowering an effect on the operations of the police department as football has on a high school.

There is no doubt that competitive athletic programs have a positive impact on communities, especially rural communities where community life often revolves around Friday night games. Participation on teams can have a tremendously powerful impact on the lives of young people and has the potential to help them develop life-long health habits. Moving sports programs out of public schools and into community organizations and businesses would not lessen these positive aspects of competitive sports. Rather, sports could play a larger role in community life by standing outside the public school system.

And the final score . . . Competitive athletic programs are an important part of the identity of many communities. Sporting events bring the community together in football stadiums and basketball courts in local schools. Participation in sports provides kids with opportunities to engage with adults in meaningful ways, develops habits of hard work and teamwork and builds an appetite for competition. Many of us believe that these are important qualities to instill in our children. The question is whether the public schools should be the institution that sponsors competitive athletic programs for the young. In many communities, Little League, YMCA, and YWCA programs and private organizations prepare kids to compete in swimming, karate, and other kinds of sports not offered by the local school. Asking communities to sponsor all competitive sports programs has a tremendous appeal.

Moving competitive sports into community organizations would begin to rebuild our community organizations and strengthen the link between schools and communities. It would free up teachers to teach. It would free up much needed school resources to align school programs and curricula to education standards, design tests to measure achievement, and provide for the necessary professional development for teachers. Eliminating sports from the purview of schools would be a huge first step in reinventing the way we spend our time and money in schools.

Raising student achievement must become more than a rhetorical battle cry. To date, that rhetoric has had the effect of increasing homework and providing the firepower for increased student testing. But the emphasis needs to shift: defining education standards must be accompanied by linking resource allocation in schools to those standards. In part II, we look at how to turn the rhetoric into action.

Part II

CHAPTER 5

Zero-Based Budgeting: Tool for Reform

*I*n the preceding chapters we examined the use of resources in schools today by taking a detailed look at the school day and the use of school dollars. Numerous examples from the daily life in schools and ample research evidence suggest that the school day currently is not structured for learning. For too much of the time that kids spend in school, the environment is chaotic, fragmented, and unfocused and too many resources are devoted to activities only tangentially related to student learning in core academic areas. In the previous chapter I went so far as to argue that sports needs to be managed by community groups and organizations rather than the public schools.

In a sense, this discussion drew a line in the sand: remove from schools those things that do not contribute to student learning as identified by the education standards developed in each state. To date, standards have been used to drive curriculum decisions, instructional patterns, and changes in how assessment is carried out. In addition, teacher professional development has been linked to the needs created by learning standards. Yet resource allocation—expenditures in time and money—has yet to be aligned with education standards.

I will now introduce some practical ideas and recommendations to put this general policy direction into practice. Since most of us live and work in communities where schools have not been restructured, we want to know ways that we can have an impact on our children's schools tomorrow. We don't want to wait for a systemwide restructuring effort before our schools improve, although we may well want to know how to lobby for those changes as well. Chapter 5 presents a zero-based budgeting exercise that most communities can undertake in order to radically revise the way they think about and spend money and align with new educational performance goals. Chapter 6 analyzes alternative ways to organize the school day and makes other recommendations on ways that schools, parents, and communities can spend time in a more thoughtful, coherent way in schools. For the most part, these ideas would cost schools nothing and are designed to give them the kind of support needed to make structural changes. In conclusion, I explore the concept of the classroom as sacred space, arguing for a rethinking of the basic metaphors that we use when talking about schools. In this way I will leave the world of policy analysis and research reports aside and talk directly to parents and teachers as if education mattered.

Recently, school finance officers in Florida told researchers that in their experience, dissemination of data about school finances does not seem to mobilize the public's interest in school improvement.[1] That will come as no surprise to anyone who has ever tried to make sense of a school budget. Few parents could take the time to work their way through any current school budget in this country. Obscure, unclear, and undifferentiated, school budgets do little to help noneducators gain clarity as to how school resources are being allocated. Consequently, even citizens who would in principle be interested in these issues find that budget documents are an obstacle to engagement. In the days of the unchallenged status quo, school budgets are not the focus of much attention in a community. But at times of change—and budget cuts—the school budget can and should be the terrain on which communities redefine their values in relation to education and structure their schools to reflect those values.

The midseventies in California were just such a time. California schools were facing mounting pressure from a number of sources.

Increased demands to serve all students, calls for equalizing school funding, and a taxpayer revolt all put the schools on notice that the status quo was in question. State lawmakers were busy designing new legislation, Assembly Bill 65, which called for school improvement and funding equalization, an equitable funding of all schools. At the heart of the bill were the radical ideas that schools should serve all students well and that state funding formulas could actually be instrumental in equalizing school funding. When Assembly Bill 65 was passed, wealthy districts lost a percentage of their tax revenue to poorer districts.

At the same time, the taxpayers of the state were calling for slashing their tax bills. Proposition 13, the first so-called "taxpayer revolt" in the country, passed—even though there were dire predictions that schools could lose up to one third of their state funding. School budgets did indeed get slashed, but in the first year after passage of the bill the shortfall was made up by a state surplus. But the writing was on the wall: Assembly Bill 65 demanded that, Proposition 13 notwithstanding, all districts were going to have to do better for all their students. In fact, the long-term effects of Proposition 13 on the schools have been staggering to a state that prior to the 1970s had a public education system second to none in the United States. State colleges and universities were virtually free and were some of the finest institutions of higher education in the world. In post–Proposition 13 California, students in state colleges and universities pay relatively high tuition rates and in some of them it takes students five years to graduate because of overcrowded classrooms. In public schools in the state, the effects of Proposition 13 were swift and immediate: draconian cuts to programs and staff threatened to leave many California schools mere shells of their former selves. This history is well known.

What is less well known is that one section of Assembly Bill 65 called for the community of parents, citizens, students, and staff to assume greater responsibility for accomplishing society's learning tasks. State lawmakers recognized that communities would have to direct their attention to restructuring how schools spend their money. The legislation mandated the establishment of "school site councils," district-level committees made up of parents, teachers, and community leaders that were charged with two tasks: to increase student academic achievement, social development, and personal growth; and to focus attention on school organization and the classroom environment. School site councils were to give attention to the coordination of resources, including staff development and parent and student involvement. In short, these councils were charged with redesigning schools to better meet students' needs and to do so with fewer resources. And they had to do this by involving the entire community. The opportunity existed for communities to set bold new directions for their schools, despite the climate created by Proposition 13. The mechanisms for designing and implementing school site councils were discussed at length on the pages of California newspapers and school publications, especially the *California School Board Journal*.

Unfortunately, there were fundamental problems with the legislation. One was that the goals for the reform were ill defined. Since the state did not have clearly articulated learning goals, each community was left to struggle with the meaning of "developing student abilities to their highest potential in basic skills and other curriculum areas, as well as in personal and social growth."[2] Just what constituted basic skills and personal and social growth became hotly contested issues in California communities. Lacking agreed-upon learning standards, communities often splintered into fractious groups competing for the right to define basic skills.

In addition, we now know that innovation mandates that emanate from the state level, especially when they are unfunded mandates, rarely take hold. School site councils were unevenly successful. In some cases, they did some good work toward restructuring their schools. In other communities, mere lip service was paid to the mandate for establishing the councils.

We can learn some lessons from the school site council era in California. One is that where there is authentic community involvement in problem-solving activities, schools get greater community support. In California communities that took the charge of the state seriously, school site councils were large and their members, committed. These councils often spun off nonprofit organizations that raised funds in their communities and picked up the tab for some of the school programs cut as a result of Proposition 13. School site councils worked closely with school boards, giving the community greater access to school decision making and a result of this was to give greater support to the local schools. Parents were in classrooms as volunteers, they helped build volunteer organizations, and they learned what kinds of roles they could play in their children's schools.

The National Education Commission on Time and Learning, established by the 1991 Education Council Act, might well have taken this page from California school history. In a 1994 report titled "Prisoners of Time," the commission had recommended a structure that sounds a lot like school site councils:

> The commission believes every community must engage in a community wide debate about the shape and future of its schools. To that end, we encourage every district, with the support of the superintendent and local school board, to engage major school stakeholders in a comprehensive, long-term dialogue about the hopes, aspirations, and future directions of local education. The conversation should include students, parents, taxpayers, employers, and representatives of public assistance, juvenile justice, health and other social services agencies.[3]

The report goes on to state that the commission's goal is to help American communities crystallize a vision for their schools, but the report lacks the details and the tools needed to structure such an undertaking. One powerful tool did, however, come out of the school site council days in California—one that could help communities conduct the kind of public conversation the commission calls for: zero-based budgeting.

Zero-Based Budgeting

As we have seen, most school budgeting processes are incremental in nature and leave basic assumptions in place: political negotiations start by taking the existing budget lines as given, and the inevitable bartering and bickering and genuine statesman-like compromise on small changes proceed from there. Zero-based budgeting represents a radical departure from this process: you could say that it asks us to start from scratch. A well-constructed zero-based budgeting process asks us to start by articulating our goals for education, and then work from there to decisions about how to spend money best—not to horse-trade about incremental changes to preexisting individual budget lines. Zero-based budgeting acknowledges that much of the school budget is determined by federal, state, and local mandates as well as union-negotiated salaries, but the process provides communities a way to make decisions about the portion of the school budget that is not set. Zero-based budgeting is a tool applied by economists in a variety of domains to lead to more rational and productive budget decisions.

A chief architect of a zero-based budgeting process applied to schools in California was Ron Chilcote, professor of political science at the University of California, Riverside. According to Chilcote, a member of the Laguna Beach Unified School Board from 1974 to 1984, zero-based budgeting begins with the simple question "What should be in the school budget?"[4] Although zero-based budgeting was not a new idea, it had never been used before in school budget decision making and it had real appeal for communities struggling with budget decisions in the face of decreased state funding and the demand to develop student abilities to their highest potential, however ill defined the goal was.

The question "What should be in the school budget?" is really a question about community values; it leads a community into discussions about the purposes and aims of education. Rather than asking the community how to cut a certain number of dollars from the existing budget, a zero-based budgeting process takes us back to the drawing board to think anew about school programs, their price, and their place in the overall curriculum and co-curricular offerings of a school. Well over 60 percent of any school budget is determined by prescribed formulas and salaries negotiated by unions. Many educators claim that another 30 percent represents fixed costs. Most schools have not done the work of rethinking their resource allocation in terms of new education standards; consequently it is hard to know how many of the "fixed costs" are really "fixed." Communities can make significant decisions about how to spend the remaining school budget, much more so than we commonly acknowledge. Zero-based budgeting gives a community the structure for thinking about new possibilities for reallocating school spending. By disconnecting a discussion of the budget from the existing budget categories, communities can begin to align the school budget to contemporary community goals and to education standards developed in their state.

Zero-based budgeting, as used in Laguna Beach in the late seventies, included building a community guide to the budget and allowing for extensive community input into the budgeting process. In community forums around town, parents shared their hopes and dreams for their children's education and learned to think about educational options in terms of opportunity costs. Learning that the budget is a constructed document that contains trade-offs and compromises was an important step in the education of parents for authentic participation. Today, in addition to a community guide to the budget, schools must help parents understand state and local learning standards.

A zero-based budgeting process today would include three distinct stages:

1. Gathering and providing information
2. Community discussion
3. Construction of two guides: a community guide to the budget and a community guide to education standards

The Community Guide to the Budget

The community guide to the budget helps the community understand the myriad budget categories and line items that make up a local school budget. In order for the public to move beyond thinking about the budget in terms of their own pet programs and their own children's favorite activity, parents must have access to clear, accurate information about the school budget as a whole. Preparing a detailed guide to the school budget shows that the need to educate the public is being taken seriously and helps parents weigh the costs of particular programs.

As we have seen, school budgets, excessively detailed, often obscure rather than clarify how the school dollar is spent. A further factor, in the case of large urban school districts, is that budgets are not detailed down to the level of the individual school but rather show expenditures for the district as a whole, which might include dozens of separate schools.[5] A zero-based budgeting exercise forces an accounting at the individual school level. This process allows everyone to have the information that has been lacking and forces schools to take seriously their responsibility to inform the public about their use of public resources.

Those who draw up school budgets do not intentionally design them to be misleading, but the ways that we have historically constructed school budgets has not led to a budgeting process that encourages close analysis, which is necessary if the public is to be involved in making hard decisions about school dollars. School budgets are confusing not only because the accounting system used in some districts aggregates the data from different schools, rendering it useless as a decision-making instrument at the individual school level, but also because expenses themselves are aggregated into categories that can appear arbitrary. In addition, program costs are often tucked away in a variety of line items in a budget. Ascertaining the full cost of competitive athletic programs is a case in point. Insurance costs, field and gym maintenance, uniform expenses for sports may be invisible because subsumed under general categories—in fact, many school administrators simply do not know the full costs of these programs in part because of accounting procedures as well as the fact that no one has asked for an accounting. Surely parents who are supporters of school-sponsored athletics would want to know the cost of what they support. In addition, if schools are to shift the responsibility of sports to community organizations, those organizations will need to know the real costs of the programs.

Demanding that a budget be broken down into categories that make sense is an art, not a formula. The community guide makes the budget more user-friendly by providing the public with information they need to fully understand the terminology and categories of a school budget, and this helps the public understand the actual cost of school programs. Asking school officials to prepare a community guide can give communities information they need to become informed participants in school decision making. Parents must hold school administrators accountable for providing accurate and detailed information about expenses. Administrators are used to having to sell the school budget. They have become good at outlining the cost to each taxpayer of any school budget increase. What they have not been good at is presenting to the public the opportunity costs of the highly visible "sideshows" of education. Fielding a winning football team with lots of coaches comes at the expense of smaller classes and more advanced course offerings. Communities need to know what these trade-offs are, and in order to find out, they need to support and lobby administrators and board members to construct a guide that really is a budget guide and not a justification for existing priorities.

Community Guide to Learning

Just as the community guide to the budget provides information necessary for community members to participate fully in a discussion of educational costs, a guide to learning standards prepares parents and interested community members to participate in educational decision making in their community. In most states education standards have been adopted, and most of these states have developed content standards—the specifics of what students should know and be able to do at various levels of their education—which that state considers the foundation to be learned. Content standards can help communities shape the school program, and in a zero-based budgeting process they help communities align their school budgets with state education standards. Aligning resources with standards is a necessary but difficult step that is usually ignored by the standards movement in this country.

A community guide to learning standards must include a full itemization of the state learning standards. Luckily most states have developed citizens' guides to standards, which can be found on the state government web site under the Department of Education. If your state does not have a user-friendly guide to standards, take the matter up with the lead education official in your state. A letter writing campaign to local papers in the state is also a good way to get the attention of state lawmakers.

Aligning budget decisions to state standards can be done by community members as they engage in a zero-based budgeting process. Not only would it begin a process whereby communities actually *use* the education standards that most states have invested heavily in; it could rationalize the budgeting process. For example, most states have standards in art education, yet when school districts begin to look for programs to cut, they often look first at art programs. The only way to hold schools accountable for offering programs that prepare students to meet educational standards is for active community members to demand this.

School boards and administrators engaged in zero-based budgeting are responsible for building the community guides to school budgeting and education standards. When the guides have been prepared and distributed, there are three essential steps in a zero-based budgeting exercise: Information gathering, study sessions, and budget construction.

More Information Gathering

When a community embarks on a zero-based budgeting process, they begin by gathering the information needed to make informed decisions about how to improve their schools. The guides to the budget and to education standards are necessary data for that process, but are by no means sufficient for the kind of study sessions communities must engage in during a zero-based budgeting exercise.

Zero-based budgeting committees must in addition gather detailed information on resource allocations in the schools. This information-gathering phase will take some dedication by community members. Existing parent-teacher organizations might be willing to take on a zero-based budgeting exercise as their major event for the year. Other volunteer organizations might be willing to step in to help with the information-gathering process. Local schools of education always have students who are looking for projects to do in the schools. We will have to be creative about finding the help needed to engage in the information-gathering phase of zero-based budgeting.

Given the dual emphasis I have given to time and money in schools, it will come as no surprise that I think this fact-finding mission must focus on the use of time in schools. Why is a time analysis crucial? Let's take as an example a currently popular activity in schools—fund-raising by students. Companies help schools raise money by providing wrapping paper or candy bars or popcorn for the kids to sell. The school gets 50 percent of the profit and the company gets the other 50 percent back. We'll set aside for the time being the significant question of the whether the company's garnering 50 percent of the earnings is profiteering or not, to ask: What portion of the school year does this activity consume? Is the money raised enough to offset the time the activity takes away from core academic learning? School administrators often tell me that it is the parents who want to have these kinds of activities in their schools. And they multiply. Parents need to know the cost of these activities in lost learning time. These kinds of questions must be asked of every activity that goes on in schools. During this past year the following activities in my local elementary school took time and resources from learning in core academic areas: children's in-school birthday parties hosted by the parents, celebration of holidays and "seasonal" events, self-esteem–building activities like "trust circles," fund-raising in preparation for class trips, fund-raising for victims of 9/11, fund-raising for Ricky Craven charities. . . .

Lest I sound like the grinch who stole Christmas with this critique, let me reemphasize that my principal aim is to reconnect the purpose of public schools with the activities of the school day. One principal told me that his primary-level teachers spend as much time in "celebrations" as they do in reading instruction. Naturally we all want our children to like school and to have a good experience, but that is best achieved by helping students be successful in school. A solid educational experience at school with lots of time for students to do their schoolwork would mean that when kids get home they could spend quality time with their friends and their parents. As things stand now, schools try to do all sorts of activities to meet the needs of the "whole child" and relegate too much important teaching to parents in the form of homework. Looking at how time is spent in school would yield some very amazing insights for us all.

Time-related questions really focus on two main issues: How much time do schools have and how do they spend it? In many ways, time is the most flexible asset that schools have to increase student learning, so analyzing time use in schools is really an exercise in asset mapping. In many respects this is a new way of thinking about what happens in school. Although restructuring time use in schools has been near the top of all school reformers' lists of recommendations for the past twenty years, how to do it has been strangely missing from the reform agenda. The strategy I describe here is one that any community with the will to improve student learning can engage in.

Any discussion of how time is used in schools must begin with an analysis of how the school day is structured. Gather information on the following time-use factors in your fact-finding mission:

What time does school start and end? Recent sleep research suggests that adolescents are on a different biological clock than adults. Some school districts have pushed forward the start time for high school until 9:00, when kids are actually awake. This is an example of decision making to support student learning.

What is the rationale for the time schedule in your school? Study groups really need to investigate this particular issue. Often the schedules are developed "backward": they start with the time demands of the afternoon sports program, and the regular class time has to be fitted in before sports practice starts. Districts with busing programs must use the same buses for all schools, and they have elaborate schedules that are often driven by the need for high school to end by 2:30 in order for athletic teams to have long afternoon practices before dark. Study groups need to determine why the school day in their community is set within the time parameters that it is. Often the length of the school day is worked out in negotiations with unions, but rarely the actual time that the day starts and ends.

How much time during the school day is given over to activities unrelated to core academic learning as outlined in the state's learning standards? For example, the fund-raising activities like selling wrapping paper to raise money for school trips? Or the drug education done by the local police? And the "specials" like AIDS education, self-esteem building, and computers that consume much of the afternoon in some elementary schools?

Is a particular activity essential for the development of core academic competencies as outlined in the state learning standards? How much time out of the school day and year is taken over by athletic events? Pep rallies? Away games?

Should a special activity be part of a regular class? For example, AIDS education is often a stand-alone "special" for older elementary, middle, and early high school students, but instead it could and should be part of the regular health class. Computer use is best taught in the context of a subject area.

Does the school-day schedule reflect the learning needs of students or the time requirements of after-school activities?

When an analysis of time use in schools is called for, it is important to stress that the implication is *not* that schools waste time and community members must come in to "fix" the problem. Rather, this exercise is designed to help parents and community members understand how their calls for new programs impact the total school program. Schools respond to pressure from the community. Local school boards can exert a tremendous amount of control over school programs. Bringing to the public's attention the ways that time gets used in school will help parents understand the true costs of the programs that they themselves often demand. Schools are getting buried under the good intentions of parents and community groups. Parents need to understand that when they bring those cupcakes into their child's first-grade class for a little birthday party, they are actually taking precious learning time away from the teacher. And let's not forget that the work ultimately comes home to the parents in the form of homework. As a matter of fact, when the community looks hard at time use in schools. it will help educators get the support they need for the whole community to rethink how the time is actually used.

Time-use and budget analysis go hand in hand when both take place under the overarching framework of learning standards. Analyzing how time is used in schools will point to large digressions from core learning, and help set priorities for budget cuts and reassignments.

Community Discussion

With the fact-finding mission complete, a guide to the school budget and state learning standards in hand, communities can engage in discussions as well-informed citizens. These sessions are an opportunity for community members to discuss how time and money are spent in the schools. Study sessions give communities the opportunity to take the public pulse, as it were, about education in the community.

Providing information to and gathering input from parents is the goal of community discussions. These sessions provide an opportunity to survey the community. In Laguna Beach the meetings occurred in the homes of interested parents and provided an opportunity for informal discussion among diverse community members. Open information meetings can be held, surveys can be distributed to parents and students, and local cable stations can host call-in shows to gather opinions. A Web site can be designed that links to local school Web sites where community members can register their views. Schools can offer chat rooms for parents and students. The key here is to have a variety of ways in which people can participate so that many community voices are heard. Typically community participation in our schools involves a small but active group of parents. This group of parents attends meetings, hosts school events, and provides the community input at board meetings. Turning around our public schools is going to require the participation of more than the usual suspects! All parents must be included and feel that their voices matter or at least get heard.

Community discussions can be communitywide events designed to attract a broad group of parents. Baby-sitting should be provided so that all parents can attend. Food helps. Someone who has experience in facilitating large meetings best facilitates these types of community sessions. In some communities, the mayor might want to devote a Saturday afternoon to such an event. Often local corporations will lend one of their meeting managers to the community. These sessions can be taped and shown on the local cable station.

The input gathered at the study sessions, from surveys, and from the web site must be synthesized and made public. Posting findings around town says to the public, we are serious about school change. Gathering input at study sessions is only the first part of the process.

These sessions will not be easy. When it comes to education, there are many opposing views, often passionately held. But the sessions are important for a number of reasons. They force the school leaders to clarify their budgets and to disclose the full costs of school programs. They help parents understand the cost of school programs in terms of both time and money. And they help decision makers become better informed about what the community wants from its schools.

Once the community has had an opportunity to participate in

the activities of zero-based budgeting, the school board has ample material for engaging in a thorough analysis of the school budget. Starting with standards that identify what students need to know and be able to do, boards can begin to align resource allocation with the learning activities designed to get our students where we want them to be. Again, these sessions will be difficult. Entrenched interests will want to protect certain programs. Unions will fight to keep their daily schedules the same.

How can a community find time for this kind of process? Parents are indeed stretched to the limit these days. More are working longer hours and some are working two jobs. But even the most overworked parents take time to attend their child's soccer game or drama event. Reviewing guides and taking an afternoon to learn about how your local school spends its time and money has got to be a high priority for all parents concerned about the learning opportunities in their local school and about the way their tax dollars get spent. Exercising local control of schools is a time-consuming, complicated way to run them. School systems in countries that control all schools from a national office are more efficient and—judging by international test score comparisons—more effective. If we are going to maintain local control of schools, we must begin to take it seriously.

Local control of schools has never been systematically supported in this country. School board members are poorly prepared for their role. They receive little training, and what training is available to them is designed by state organizations and is often poorly attended. Pressure comes at school board members from all directions and board members often just try to keep their heads above water. Entrenched school programs continue in the face of new knowledge about how to improve schools for increased learning. Activities that could be sponsored and supported by community-based organizations continue to eat up school resources because communities have not had the mechanism to engage in reprioritizing the allocation of their resources. Nor have they had the intestinal fortitude for the debate. Engaging in a zero-based exercise is one way for communities to regain their schools and to redirect school resources to activities that contribute to higher academic achievement.

In some communities, local schools have restructured themselves using principles outlined in the literature of one of the many national organizations that facilitate school restructuring. For most communities, interested teachers and parents will have to initiate the process of improving their schools. The work will be hard. Luckily, there are roadmaps. The best roadmap, especially for elementary school restructuring for learning, is Linda Darling-Hammond's *The Right to Learn* (1997). This book is essential reading for community leaders serious about improving educational achievement in their communities. There are also land mines: the vested interests in communities that will protect their turf against any challenge. The zero-based budgeting exercise outlined above gives communities a way to become informed, gather information and study that information before going into a budget-setting session where the vested groups will be out in full force. Armed with information, communities can make better-informed decisions to redirect their school programs so that all schools can come closer to an ideal of the school as a sacred space where learning is the top priority, to which all resources are directed.

Looking at a guide to the budget developed by another community can give us an idea of what kinds of information communities need to understand and reconstruct the school budget. Information on budget line items—which ones are mandated by law and which ones are flexible—is essential. The first community budget guides were developed in the seventies; today in many communities the school budget is much more detailed and has more set categories. Nevertheless there is still an opportunity to make significant decisions about how the school dollar is spent, especially in athletics.

What Can Communities Do?

Zero-based budgeting begins with the deceptively simple question "What should be in the budget?" In imagining communities asking this question, I have been imagining a particular approach to the larger background democratic question "What should schools be in the business of doing?" Indeed, I am asking communities to self-consciously ask what children and families need from schools at a time when the lines between community and school are being redrawn by a variety of social forces.

The American family has changed dramatically in the past thirty years. We have many more single-parent families than we did in the seventies. In the majority of families with two parents, both parents work. For the first time in history, the majority of mothers work outside the home. The average family today has twenty-two fewer hours to spend each week at home than did families thirty years ago.[6] As communities around the country face staggering social changes, schools are often called upon and compelled to respond in a variety of ways. Our progressive legacy dictates that schools should respond to these changes. One such response has been the growth of the full-service community school model. This conception envisions the school as a safe, welcoming neighborhood hub that is open from early in the morning until late at night, serving as a community center and baby-sitting service. Community schools offer homework help, medical and dental care, and a whole variety of enrichment programs.

A number of national organizations—one example is the Coalition for Community Schools—provide technical and startup support to keep school buildings open longer hours and provide a vast array of support services. Communities-in-schools brings the business community into partnership with local schools to provide community services in schools. The rise of after-school programs and the growth of the full-service community school model have overshot all expectations. Funding by the U.S. Department of Education's 21st Century Community Learning Centers went from $1 million in 1997 to more than $800 million in 2001. At least 26 states intend to increase funding for extra learning opportunities.[7] The United Way has been active in building partnerships between schools and nonprofit agencies to integrate education with human- and community-service delivery systems and to transform schools into lifelong learning centers and community hubs. Foundations, notably the Charles Stewart Mott Foundation and the DeWitt Wallace–Readers Digest Fund, have supplied millions of dollars for the support of research, development, and replication of community-service schools. In 1986, the Children's Aid Society began its community school program, which helps community agencies partner with schools to offer school-based primary health care providers, mental health workers, and extended academic support.

The move to integrate service delivery systems into one community center and to network the resources of communities is certainly a welcome change. Housing these services in schools makes sense to many community leaders. After all, no one liked seeing the school buildings empty in the late afternoon and evening. Despite their positive aspects, however, these programs raise significant questions for school communities struggling to meet state learning standards in order to increase academic achievement in their students.

Do we stretch the ability of school personnel beyond their limit when we add to their already overcrowded job the responsibility to network and build a community center in their school after hours? How do we compensate teachers for the work of ensuring the academic quality of after-school help offered to students? Marge Scherer, editor-in-chief of *Education Leadership,* a key publication for school leaders, reminds us, "Whether schools should extend their primary duty—to educate all students—to include offering after-school care is still a matter of debate."

Scherer's skepticism points to the central thesis of this book. If we intend to increase student achievement to any significant degree, schools must give their complete attention to student learning. Full-service community schools have caught on because there is a crying need for community service centers that provide a variety of services to young and old alike. From the point of view of maximizing student learning, however, schools may in fact not be the best locus for full-service community centers.

Why not full-service communities? School resources are already stretched just to provide the necessary academic support for student learning. School *buildings* might house community centers that provide necessary services to community members, but asking school *personnel* to take a leadership role in designing, finding funding for, and managing such an undertaking may not be the best use of their time.

Some districts draw a clear line between these necessary social services and the activities related to the academic school day as they try to overcome the fragmented school experience that plagues many of our nation's children. Narrowing the focus of our schools by aligning resource allocation with state learning standards gives a community the opportunity to rein in an educational system that is overflowing its natural boundaries. This does not mean that communities that have broader goals for the health of their children need to turn their backs on these services, but rather that schools alone cannot and should not have to shoulder the burden of providing them.

Many other community organizations can take up the slack as schools pull back in their mission and focus on their core goals. Faith-based organizations currently enjoy the opportunity to compete for federal funds. These organizations often suffer from having to compete with schools to provide community services. Community organizations such as YMCAs and YWCAs and boys and girls clubs, which suffer from lack of membership, could be restructured to participate more fully in building full-service communities.

In a zero-based budgeting exercise, communities can distinguish between core learning goals that form the mission of the school system, as reflected in a state's education standards, and the broader social goals of the community, which can easily be agreed upon but which cannot and should not compete with the scarce resources allotted to schools. I don't what to make my recommendations for zero-based budgeting sound easy or merely procedural. In fact, I see it as a tool for examining and radically changing our priorities. In arguing that schools should do less—so that they can concentrate more completely on their core mission, learning—I am arguing for a major shift in our expectations of schools. This requires a major shift in the way we determine how to use the resources we have.

A zero-based budgeting exercise helps parents come to know the true costs of the programs they would like to see in their schools. It brings us back to the drawing board by forcing us to ask fundamental questions about our schools. And it provides communities with a way to rethink how they deliver services to the young. In the next chapter, we will look at some specific models for other ways to spend school days and dollars.

CHAPTER 6

Restructuring Time, Restructuring Schools: Recommendations for Unburdening Schools

*A*s Alexandra drives up to Willard High School, she glances at the Willard bulletin board to check out the thought for the week:

Each generation must, out of relative obscurity, discover its mission, fulfill it or betray it. Frantz Fanon, 1959

Alexandra knows that her English teacher will spend a few minutes talking about the quote, so she begins to think about who might have said such a thing as she tries to find a parking place. It's almost nine o'clock and Alexandra has already had early-morning swim practice, followed by soccer practice. She feels awake and ready to start the school day.

As Alexandra makes her way to her morning class, she notices the computer screens in the halls, reminders about the community play this weekend and the extended hours for the resource room. Since Willard replaced the loudspeakers in the classrooms with computer monitors in the hallways displaying messages that update students about important events, Alexandra is able to pick and choose what to pay attention to.

Arriving at class, Alexandra inserts her ID card in the box inside the classroom door. A computerized message is sent to the office that she is in fact entering the classroom. Her morning class begins with a discussion of the Fanon quote. Her teacher likes to get the students "warmed up," as she calls it, before they jump into the work of the day.

After a few minutes' discussion about Frantz Fanon and his work, Alexandra's teacher asks whether his quote has any meaning for us in the United States? The discussion gets heated as the students begin to suggest what the mission of their generation might be. In the old days, this warm-up time was spent on taking attendance and listening to loudspeaker announcements. But now, ten minutes into a ninety-minute class, most students are engaged learners. The later, 9:00, start time means that few students are struggling to stay awake in the back of the class. Since the students are presenting their projects on the Heart of Darkness, not everyone needs to be in class. Students not presenting their projects on this day check out of class and go to one of the many resource rooms around the school to work on projects, while the day's presenters remain in class and serve as an audience. Alexandra is not selected for today, so she slips out of her seat, inserts her ID card into the attendance box, and heads for a resource room. In the old days there were no workspaces in the school where students could work independently; today the school is filled with resource rooms where students do their schoolwork. Today, Alexandra uses the computers to get the material she needs to finish her science project. She sends an instant message to her science team to see if anyone is doing independent work somewhere in the school. In a minute she hears back that one member is in the science lab recording observation notes. Alexandra finishes downloading a graph and heads to the science lab to help her teammate with observations.

With ninety-minute class periods, students have a ten-minute passing period between classes. The halls are still filled with the energy that hundreds of adolescents generate, but the pushing and shoving has diminished somewhat because the students have more time to get to their next class. Alexandra's second class period of the day lasts until her lunch period. In the afternoon, she has her third, or block 3, class and then an hour and a half of tutorial time, during which she can work with teachers on her course work and independent projects. At the beginning of the tutorial period, Alexandra logs onto her portfolio "to do" list to make sure that she hasn't forgotten some long-term project that she needs to work on. She sees that she needs to check with her English teacher about comments on her last paper. Alexandra spends the afternoon rewriting her *Heart of Darkness* paper and heads off to her teacher's office to talk about the relation of the quote for the week that is on the Willard bulletin board and the theme of the book. They have to be connected, thinks Alexandra, but she isn't sure how.

Five years ago Willard went through a communitywide school reform process that began after a zero-based budgeting process identified sources of grave concern in the community over the culture of the school. After a long year of community meetings, focus groups, work groups, consulting input, and grant writing, the Willard community decided on a course of action.

The first change that was instituted was to move to a schedule of three courses a day taught in longer blocks of time. These courses meet every day for close to three months, at which time students have completed what used to be a yearlong course. This trimester system allows students to complete nine courses over the length of the school year. The school instituted a tutorial system whereby teachers were available to work individually with students. It also installed a wireless local area network that allows students to access their portfolios, digital books, course-work notes from teachers, and the Internet. Students can do real-time group work in a chat room as well as meet informally in cluster areas around the school.

The school redesigned much of the teaching space into resource rooms. These learning spaces have computers hooked up to the Internet, small discussion spaces, and an aide who oversees the space. Newspapers, reference materials, and plants give the space a welcoming feeling of seriousness as students enter. For the most part, teachers became coaches and mentors, helping students construct new knowledge through the retrieval, synthesis, and management of information from an endless variety of sources. Senior seminars replaced most of the course work of the senior year. These seminars were designed to build learning communities where students could engage with one another about their individual research projects, share insights gleaned from their internships in the community, or participate in any one of a number of advanced-study seminars designed by students.

The second major change in Willard was that community groups stepped forward to take responsibility for extracurricular activities. For example, the school no longer sponsors the drama program, which is now conducted under the auspices of a local bank; it uses the school facility at night and includes members from the community. To everyone's surprise, the plays are much better when both adults and children take roles rather than having high school–age students made up to look old. Sports practice, once done after school, now takes place early in the morning before school. The police department has taken over the football team and the chamber of commerce runs soccer. Scheduling practices and times for games was not easy and there was lots of grumbling, but now the community points with pride to "their" teams, because they truly are "their" teams. Community members who had never been part of the school sports program now enjoy participating as coaches or timekeepers. For the students at Willard High School, this change has meant that a new culture exists at the school.

A good part of Alexandra's new day at school looks like the days in some restructured schools around the country. Block schedules —where class periods previously devoted to different subject areas are combined to produce time blocks, longer continuous stretches of time—are becoming more common. By some estimates, close to 30 percent of high schools in the United States have moved to some form of block scheduling. Block schedules make better sense for teaching because teachers see fewer students in a day. Completing the course work for a year in a concentrated time period means that students can really focus on learning a particular subject. Despite these pluses, Joseph Carroll, credited with being the "father of the block schedule," warns that it is not a magic bullet.[1] In addition, resistance to the block schedule by teachers, unions, and communities should alert us to the fact that school change cannot be done piecemeal. Asking teachers to move from 42-minute to 90-minute periods only makes sense if the change is accompanied by a paradigm shift in the way we think about teaching and learning.

Communities do not need to go it alone when it comes to redesigning their schools. A number of dynamic organizations have come into being with the aim of facilitating school change. The Coalition of Essential Schools (CES), a national network of schools, centers, and a national office working to rebuild and restructure schools, has provided the most systematic thinking about educational change and support for school change. This organization supports a vast network of restructured schools—also called "essential" schools—around the country and has developed a systematic approach to school restructuring. A key principle of restructured schools in the coalition is "Less is more." CES schools build for deeper learning of fewer subjects. Their web site (www.ces.org) is filled with resources for understanding the relation of time use to student learning. Hundreds of "essential schools" around the country are showing every day that when you put student learning at the center of school planning you arrive at a very different place than a traditional school.

California Tomorrow, an organization helping schools better meet the needs of immigrant students, advocates the use of block scheduling for meeting the needs of a diverse-language student body.[2] They too acknowledge that changing the schedule is only one part of what must be a multilayered approach to school reform.

Even strong advocates for block scheduling warn that doubling class periods must be accompanied by essential changes in the ways we think about the work of teaching and learning.[3] Better use of technology, an examination of the place of extracurricular activities in the school day, and opportunities for teachers to understand and practice their work in new ways must all accompany any reform item. Looking at Alexandra's day, we see that teachers and students are working in new ways; technology is used to make the school day more efficient and to make learning richer; academic work does not compete with sports for student attention; and in general her school has become more focused on learning and less focused on "the sideshows of education."

What Is to Be Done?

Alexandra's reimagined school day is a sketch of a school that, instead of doing trying to do too much, does fewer things but a better job of the things we care most about. This thought experiment can help us imagine much more. We must begin to unburden the public schools of activities that are not central to their teaching mission, a process that will allow teachers to devote more of their time and energy to creating richer, more robust learning environments in our schools. To reach that goal there are very specific steps that communities can take. The recommendations below are premised on a very straightforward idea: the need to recalibrate the relationship between the school and the community. This is not just a rhetorical statement: in very concrete ways the community must support student learning by taking some of the load off the schools. It is now widely acknowledged that increasing student learning must become the responsibility of all elements of a community.[4] What has been missing is a public conversation about how to do that.

The schools for their part must take a leadership role by putting aside the distractions that interrupt the school day; simultaneously, the community must be willing to acknowledge its role in expecting schools to do too much. We have seen how fund-raising activities, community service education, and sports—activities only tangentially related to learning in the core academic subject areas—all have taken a chunk out of the learning day so that now learning has to go home in the form of homework.

All stakeholders in the educational enterprise of a community can contribute to constructive change. The measures described below can do wonders to refocus the attention of the school on teaching and learning and to help communities understand their responsibility for the education of their children. The recommendations are very specific and for the most part can be carried out without increased funding to schools. They can be put in place without waiting for state or federal approval. They do not require a team of "experts" for successful completion. I have left off my list of recommendations school reform components that are already well known—to me, that class sizes need to be smaller; that teachers need more time for professional development; that schools need the necessary resources to make full use of technology to increase student learning and teacher efficiency are all givens. Many of the books listed in "Selected Readings" discuss these well-known issues fully.

In the rest of this chapter you will encounter fresh, commonsense ideas that have come to me from parents, teachers, and administrators around the country who have shared their hopes and frustrations about the state of their public schools. They are culled from national reports and research findings that don't often make their way out of educational research journals. They reflect my own experiences teaching and raising children who attended numerous public schools across the country and my years of sitting in school board meetings and running community meetings for parents.

These ideas for constructive engagement and action come from looking at schools and realizing that they *can* be otherwise than what they are, looking at the possible instead of the given. They grow out of the current realities of schooling yet challenge passive acceptance of what schools today are. These initiatives are also radical in that they ask the community to share the responsibility for the rituals of schooling and for changing these rituals. They call on communities to rethink their relationship to their schools. In addition, they ask the community to become involved in the education of the young in an authentic and significant way. When communities take a more active role in increasing educational opportunities, not only do they unburden the public schools but also, the shift allows professional educators to do the job they were trained to do. My recommendations for action will help flagging communities rebuild themselves by demanding more from each citizen. Warning: These measures are not for the weak-willed; they are not a restatement of well-known components of school reform. They break new ground.

Break-the-mold schools are being designed in many places in this country. But without break-the-mold thinking, these schools often do more of the same, though they do it somewhat better. Authentic change demands that we rethink school practices and rituals, never an easy task. But if we are indeed to reach higher academic standards and prepare our students for work in the twenty-first century as well as active citizenship in a democratic society, it will take more than business as usual.

What School Leadership Can Do

ELIMINATE THE "SIDESHOWS"

School principals should take steps to move athletic and drama programs outside the purview of the public school and into the community. To do this they should encourage the creation of a community group charged with building community-based athletics and drama programs. As controversial as this is, getting competitive athletics out of the school and off the school budget will be the single most significant change a school can make toward changing the culture of schools and increasing academic achievement. Taking the competitive athletic program out of the public schools frees up resources for learning and sends the message that we are serious about learning. It redirects teacher attention to learning. Relocating drama and sports in the community will enrich community life and encourage broader interest in and responsibility for the activity.

After the initial grumbling and community outcry, principals can structure this process as a "win/win" situation for communities. Schools will need to outline the exact costs of athletic programs before they go to the community. Constructing a "Community Guide to the School Budget" will help the community understand the enormous cost of athletics and why the after-school athletic program needs to be organized and run by some community entity other than the public school. This is not to say that the school facilities shouldn't be used by an organization that runs the community's athletic program. Playing fields, locker rooms, and gyms already exist, so we should use them, but those in a community who are interested in maintaining competitive athletic offerings for the young should take over the task of running the programs.

There are a number of candidates for taking over sports programs. In some places, the YMCA/YWCA will be a natural community sponsor; in others existing Little League organizations could be expanded to include other sports. In other settings, businesses could each take on a particular sport, or a major business in the community might be inspired to take over the entire program. School budgets could be aligned with state learning standards and freed from the hidden costs of running competitive athletic programs for the community's enjoyment. Indeed, the sports program is one program that other community organizations are likely to be able to pick up and run effectively. It is not possible to ask a bank to take over the math program in a school, but it is possible and highly desirable to ask a bank to sponsor a sports team.

However it is done, eliminating "sideshows" will have major benefits for children's education. Schools will be able to refocus their physical education programs to serve all students. With competitive athletics out of the purview of the school, the culture of sports, which permeates most high schools today, can slowly shift to a culture of learning.

Meanwhile, making this cultural shift will build community as well. Communities want to be involved in their schools but have few avenues where their participation is authentic and supportive. Business leaders speak at public meetings about their support of schools, but have few avenues for action. Community members often complain of being alienated from schools. But if businesses and community organizations run competitive athletic programs, more members of the community have a stake in these activities. Business leaders might need to give employees who participate support and develop flexible work schedules to accommodate their community service. Such service can be an aspect of employees' own development as well. Asking this of our communities forces people to "put their money where their mouth is," and moves us beyond the rhetoric of school reform to the hard work of making it happen.

If the police department sponsored the football team, part of the working day of some policemen would be staffing the early-morning football practice. Discussion around the station house would be the sports schedule and an upcoming game. This would provided a foundation for authentic relationships between the police and the kids in a community. Furthermore, it would eliminate another "sideshow": the need for police to take time during the school day to conduct public relations activities in the school, which go on in many communities now. Schools could redirect this time too to learning.

Changing the way competitive athletics are offered in communities also means that school leadership has to work closely with the community on use of facilities, scheduling, and the like. This transforms the school-community relationship into one of authentic partnership and collaboration.

PHASE OUT HOMEWORK

The pedagogical value of homework is overrated; the problems it causes families are well-known and it is a black hole when it comes to accountability.[5] Eliminating homework will no doubt demand that your school begins an examination of the school schedule and will lead for calls to extend the school day. An extended day can provide teachers opportunities for collaborative work, a necessary component for professional development.

The all-important principle that should guide a redesigned schedule is that all assigned schoolwork should be completed at school, where all students have equal access to educational resources. Students should be able to go home at night knowing that they have completed a full day of rigorous academic work and that their evening can be spent participating in community events, learning on their own, and enjoying an enriched family life.

RIP OUT THE LOUDSPEAKERS

Loudspeakers are the single most disruptive element in classroom life. Loud announcements damage the classroom environment and disturb the flow of thought for teachers and students, causing students to loose focus and misdirecting their attention away from learning. In addition to the negatives of noise and distraction is a psychological downside: many loudspeaker announcements concern "in-crowd" activities and have an alienating effect on kids who don't participate in the activities that are being hawked during the school day.

Many schools have limited loudspeaker announcements to a few times during the day. Even then, they are more a disruption than an effective tool for communication. School officials need to scrutinize how they are using loudspeakers now and develop an alternative approach. Better use of technology could solve the problem of the need to inform the school community of events. Messages to both teachers and students can be sent to their computers. Schools with Channel

One could use the TV screens to run announcements during passing periods. Schools will come up with different solutions to the problem, but each school needs to face the fact that interrupting classroom learning time with announcements from the front office must become a thing of the past.

THROW OUT STUDENT FUND-RAISING

Selling popcorn, wrapping paper, or magazines to raise money takes time and student energy. Beyond that, companies that supply the products, many of whom take 50 percent of the profit generated, do not have the schools' best interest at heart. There are all kinds of things that parent groups can do to raise money, and communities can raise money through their various organizations. But teachers and students should not be taking time in the school day—or after school or at night—to do this. Furthermore, we should not build a competitive environment in the classroom that privileges better-off children. Fund-raising expectations cause kids in poor communities to suffer, while more well off kids simply hit up their relatives.

Activities of genuine educational value should be funded by communities. For example, class trips account for a bulk of the fund-raising done at school, and some of them do have important educational components. If a school deems the trip an essential part of the educational experience of its students, then the cost of that trip should be covered by the school budget. If the trip is part of a traditional end-of-the-year experience for sixth-, eighth-, or twelfth-graders, we must ask whether it has educational value or is merely "tradition." For example, in one town a trip to Disneyland is part of the celebrations of senior year. Students spend a good part of their senior year washing cars, doing bake sales and the like to raise money. All of this is organized and sponsored by the school. We need to ask whether this should be part of the school or whether it should become part of the work of the local community.

Some schools raise funds for pet projects, like the Red Cross or the World Wildlife Fund. These certainly are worthwhile organizations that need financial support, but are the schools the place where kids should raise money? Some people argue that fund-raising activities build school spirit and provide kids with a sense of the larger community, which are important and necessary traits to develop. But school spirit can better be built by building a stronger learning environment and having kids do more work together in teams. Learning to be part of a larger community is best fostered by freeing up time in the school day for school work, so that the kids are not weighed down with so much homework that they have no time for community activities.

MAKE SCHOOL A NO-CONSTRUCTION ZONE

Have work that needs to be done on the school building and grounds done after the school day or before the start of school and on weekends. The excitement of painters, the noise of lawnmowers, and pounding of hammers all compete with learning for student attention and learning will almost always lose out. Contracts for schoolwork should be awarded to companies that are willing to work outside of school hours.

KEEP THE LOCAL COMMUNITY INFORMED

Write a column in the local paper that helps inform the community about what is going on in the school. Not just the "We did this . . ." kind of column, but one dealing with the substantive issues that schools face as they try to restructure for improved student learning. This kind of public discourse helps the community learn how decisions are getting made and why. Communities need to know the demands placed on schools; they need to have information about education standards in the state and about how the school plans to meet them. School leadership must provide this kind of understanding if we are going to get everyone pulling together to improve learning opportunities in schools.

What School Board Members Can Do

SUPPORT THE SHIFT TO COMMUNITY-BASED ATHLETICS AND DRAMA

Help the school administration build a budget that identifies the full cost of the athletic program and gives an accurate accounting of the number of students involved. Provide a leadership role in articulating to the community the reasons for restructuring and the benefits to the community. Begin a conversation in your community about the issue and develop strategies to facilitate the change. This must include using your own position in the community to get all the leverage you can. School board members are often community leaders and as such have power to reshape community life. Help your own business or organization become a founding sponsor of this shift. Help find community organizations that will sponsor athletic and drama programs.

A campaign to build a community-based athletic program will have to be developed community by community and only community leaders, in collaboration with school leaders, will be able to leverage the change. Board members are in a position to offer leadership in this cause.

USE BOARD MEETINGS AS A COMMUNITY FORUM

Encourage the community to attend board meetings. Hold board meetings at night so parents can attend. School board meeting nights should be "no homework" nights, to make it easier for parents to attend. The issues raised in this book can only be addressed if we provide more public forums for communities to rethink their schools. The school board meeting is an ideal location for those conversations to begin, and they should be used to their full potential.

DEVELOP A GUIDE TO BUDGET AND LEARNING STANDARDS

Even if you don't engage in a full zero-based budgeting exercise, develop guides to the school budget and state learning standards so that parent participation is meaningful and useful. This is important not only because it makes parents better informed on educational issues, but also because bringing the community into school decision making in a more authentic way increases the support that the community is willing to give the school. The community needs better and more detailed information about matters concerning the school. Parents need a larger picture than just their own child's classroom. We want parents to be involved in the schools, but only if they have the information necessary to be involved in constructive ways.

BECOME BETTER INFORMED ABOUT EDUCATION

Attend informational meetings offered by your state organizations. Become as well informed as possible about new research on teaching and learning and begin to think of yourself as an educational leader. School decision making in the twenty-first century must be based on solid research, new thinking, and fresh ideas. The books listed in "Suggested Readings" are a good place to start your research. Discourage those people from running for the school board who you think will not take educational leadership seriously. Indeed, if you are unwilling to become an educational leader you should think twice about running for the office.

What Parents Can Do

RETHINK THE ROLE OF COMPETITIVE ATHLETICS IN SCHOOL

Become informed about the costs of the athletic program in your school and its role in the daily life of the school. Ask your kids questions about the role of sports in the life of the school. Talk to others in your community about the possibility of taking the responsibility for competitive athletics out of the school and placing it in the hands of the wider community. Talk about the possibility at your place of work. Agree to serve on a planning committee to explore the issue. Use your network to strategize ways to fund and support community-based athletics and drama programs.

GET INVOLVED!

Learn more about the schools in your community; go to school board meetings. Ask to have the school develop a "Community Guide to the School Budget" and to state learning standards so you can be informed about the cost of the programs in your child's school. Know the cost of the programs that you think should be part of the school offerings and understand what programs they are competing with for scarce funds.

LISTEN TO WHAT YOUR KIDS SAY ABOUT SCHOOL

It's always useful to talk to your children about how they spend their time in school. Don't dismiss their complaints; probe them.

When parents get involved in school, they need to have as much information as possible about the school day. Your kids are a very good source of information about school, so listen to them.

GET OTHER PARENTS INVOLVED

A group of parents can act as a support for a school that is trying to restructure for student learning. It can act as a pressure group in a community that is resistant to taking more responsibility for making school programs community-based. Talk to other parents about the importance of unburdening the school if we hope to make the changes necessary to increase student learning. The Suggested Readings list at the end of this book identifies works that would be good for parents to use in study group sessions.

RETHINK YOUR PRIORITIES

Most teachers and principals claim that parents are the ones who want big after-school sports programs, "fun activities" like celebrating children's birthdays in school, and school-sponsored fundraisers for worthy causes. As we saw earlier in this book, these things all come at a tremendous cost in terms of time and money. The demands we place on schools to provide services and programs that are outside the core mission of the public schools take a tremendous toll on student learning. This can create a conflict for teachers who take their job seriously. Do not put school personnel in the awkward position of having to choose between serious instruction in academic areas and activities that are outside the purview of a school, which is devoted to teaching and learning.

What the Community as a Whole Can Do

HELP THE SCHOOL FOCUS ON TEACHING AND LEARNING

Booster clubs could lead the way in this. Support the school efforts to redirect their resources to teaching and learning by offering to help with the restructuring efforts. Businesses could sponsor sports teams and provide release time for employees who want to get involved, community organizations like the YMCA could provide the organizational structure for community-based sports programs. Police and fire departments could help with the coaching. Community-based drama programs could replace the drama programs offered by schools, increasing the participation of the community and increasing students cross-generation interaction.

ELIMINATE INTERRUPTIONS FOR DOCTOR APPOINTMENTS

Those who provide medical, dental, and mental-health services to children and teens should change their working hours so that they can see these patients outside of school hours. Enlightened pediatricians, orthodontists, and dentists have shifted their office hours to later in the day in order to meet the needs of kids. Children who come and go during the teaching day for doctor and dentist appointments cause significant disruptions in the classroom. Psychologists in France see their teenage clients on Saturday and Sunday and in the evening.

IMPROVE LOCAL NEWSPAPER COVERAGE

Newspapers must make a greater effort to report academic achievement highlights, and not just sports events. Local newspapers should shoot for having as many pages devoted to learning as to sports. Beyond getting schools to subscribe, newspapers must begin to support student learning. Why not include an article on an interesting project done in the local middle school? An achievement of merit by a young scholar? Papers do report news about students getting special awards and the like, but I am suggesting that newspapers should cover ordinary but important academic activities engaged in by the students on a regular basis, as they cover sports events every week.

LEVERAGE LEARNING AT THE LIBRARY

Rekindle interest in the local library by increasing its technology capacity and boosting its role in the community. Library building projects enrich a community and send a clear message that the community values learning. Keep the library open at night; libraries could be open noon to eight rather than ten to five. Changing hours sends a message that the library has something of value for kids, that the community encourages kids to explore learning on their own, and provides the resources to do so.

The ecologist Bill Drury has said: "When your views on the world and your intellect are being challenged and you begin to feel uncomfortable because of a contradiction you have detected that is threatening your current model of the world, or some aspect of it, pay attention: you are about to learning something."[6]

Indeed, when we hear ways of doing school differently, we are going to get a bit uncomfortable. For example, the suggestion that schools should pass off their drama and competitive sports programs to other community organizations may make many wonder: Is that possible? The answer is a resounding yes! When it comes to re-creating our schools and communities, enormous change is possible. This is not just a slogan or wishful thinking. The local democratic structures of American schools and civic life do in fact make change possible, if we pay attention and if we will it and work on it together. We are limited only by our ability to think through the structures that have determined the way it is for so long that they seem set in stone. Yet we have hundreds of wonderful changed schools that were able to reenvision themselves, in part because they refused to believe they couldn't.

As states begin to enact education standards, vested interests are going to begin to fight against moving forward with standards-based innovation. Calling for higher education standards and restructuring our schools to meet them is going to take real change. We will all have to commit to participating in the process of improving our schools; one good place to start is to accept our responsibility to participate in this process.

CHAPTER 7

The Classroom as Sacred Space

A thing becomes sacred when humans remove it
from ordinary use.

—Émile Durkheim

*W*hen people talk about schools, the word "vision" crops up
again and again. Schools bring in experts to lead the school
community through "visioning" sessions. These experts and other
high-profile educators commonly talk about their new vision for
schooling. They spout platitudes about their vision that all students
are able to learn. But learn what? and how? and where? and when? Fu-
turists envision community learning centers housed in libraries that
are open twenty hours a day, learning on demand via the computer—
in short, life without schools as we know them. All these visions for
the future may come to fruition for the next generation, but in the
meantime we need answers about what we can do next week and next
year to improve our schools.

Leaders in educational change know that new visions have to mix
with the here and now; a vision, to be useful, has to be able to lead us
from here to there.[1] And any vision of schooling must build on the reform work that has been done in education in the past twenty years.

We have most of the major pieces of the school reform puzzle figured out; what we need now is the will to act on our knowledge.

For most of the twentieth century, schools in this country were built on a factory model. They were large regimented places that prepared students for life in industrial America. Since they were government buildings, albeit locally controlled, they were not inspirational places. They were painted with cheap industrial paint, wired with loudspeakers so administrators could assert control at any time, and filled with industrial-strength furniture, designed to withstand the constant overuse of too many students in too small a space. Teachers fought against this environment, which often seemed hostile to learning. They decorated their classrooms with bright bulletin boards and mobiles, changing the scene to fit each season, and with student work on the walls. But when the year ended and the teachers cleared out their classrooms, they were still rooms often made of cement blocks and painted depressing colors that my students liked to call monkey-vomit green.

These school structures survive and for the most part are public buildings that towns begrudgingly support and constantly complain about. Parents get involved when their kids are in them and then lose interest as their kids move on. They are poorly maintained, underfunded, and often inappropriately staffed. Most are closed at 3:30 and all summer long. Some high schools are open at night for adult education classes. In some rare cases, communities build new schools that are massive community centers offering medical and dental care and opening their swimming pools and gyms and theater to the community at large. The community may flock to sports events but rarely do they flock to public demonstrations of student learning. The largest movement in public education today is the movement out of it; the number of home-schooled students has increased dramatically in the past ten years.

We know from the past twenty-five years of school reform that the change process is hard and the work of change must be focused. The models that exist give us hope that it can be done. Education standards give us a framework toward which to direct change. However, without a new way to think and talk about schools, the vast majority of schools in this country will not be able to support increased academic achievement among the young and to reengage the next generation of citizens in learning.

The School as Sacred Space

Durkheim noted that "to call a place sacred asserts that a place, its structure, and its symbols express fundamental cultural values and principles. By giving these visible form, the sacred place makes tangible the identity of people, their world and their aspirations."[2] What would it mean if we came to think of schools as sacred space? And what could I mean by that question? The dictionary tells us that "sacred," in a nonreligious context, means dedicated or devoted exclusively to a single use, purpose, or person. Of course, when we think of sacred space religious purposes come to mind first, and we think of churches, synagogues, and mosques. These are all places whose features and uses are shaped by a publicly respected purpose. Note that purposes can be broadly defined: no one will doubt that a church's dedicated purpose is for religious worship, even though that worship might include running a day-care center, a soup kitchen, and other community services.

But we all have an idea of sacred space that goes beyond religion in any narrow sense. For some, it is a favorite river or forest. For others, it is the majesty of the Grand Canyon. Gardens provide a sacred space for many. On a national level, public monuments and commemorative sites—the Capitol, Gettysburg, the Vietnam Memorial—are secular sacred sites for many Americans. We not only dedicate these places to a specific publicly valued purpose but protect them against the intrusions of outside forces—development, the market, pollution, sale to the highest bidder.

According to the theologian Jonathan Smith, a sacred space is a "focusing lens." The space helps us focus attention on the forms, objects, and actions in it.[3] Space can be sacred during one use and nonsacred at other times. Sacred space is where we communicate with our better selves and our beliefs. Sacred spaces, I would argue, are places where our deepest values are given external form and where we cultivate those values.

How might schools be considered sacred space? What conditions do schools meet that could qualify them as sacred space?

For one, they meet Smith's conception of sacred space as a focusing lens. Schools are places where we go to focus attention on learning. As a focusing lens, schools can—and, I would argue, should—be places where all attention is directed singularly to teaching and learning. We all know that learning goes on all the time, not just in school. But schools are places where we go to make explicit what kinds of learning we value most. From a constructivist point of view, schools are places where teachers help students build new mental maps of the world they live in. At its best, teaching is about giving students the tools to interpret and shape experience in new and more powerful ways.

In the early days of our nation, children went to so-called "dame schools" to learn to read, run by women in their homes. But when students came to learn, they were in fact schools. Home-schoolers use their dining rooms as classrooms, and they actually become classrooms. The space where learning takes place has both sacred and non-sacred uses, but when formal learning occurs, it becomes a sacred learning space.

Sacredness can in its way be an impediment to change. For instance, sacred space often implies rituals, time-honored routines and ceremonies that give structure to our lives. The rituals of schooling may be deeply comforting, but they contribute to the static, difficult-to-change nature of schools. When we walk into the school, the smell of the chalk dust, the noise of the hallways during passing periods all take us back to our own childhoods. We see on the windows the colored-paper turkeys made by outlining a hand, the same turkeys we made as children. We see the same finger-painted snowmen and the list of the milk monitors. Schools still have the same long holidays. They have the same pep rallies and homecoming dances. The children are sitting in the same desks that we sat in.

One of the hard things about changing schools is that much of what goes on in them is, in fact, ritual. According to the educator Joe McDonald, transforming rituals must become one of the key activities of school leaders: "[Rituals] . . . routinely enact and reenact the school's deepest assumptions about the purpose of schooling. . . .

Through constant wear, the beliefs embedded in particular rituals may grow tacit."[4] Once tacitly accepted, rituals can become routines and lose meaning. They become mere habits, hard to break.

But I also see the metaphor of sacredness as a rich, guiding principle of positive change. In many ways, this book has been asking: How can we turn our schools into sacred space? How can schools become focusing lenses for learning? How do we re-form the rituals in schools so that they contribute to, rather than distract from, student learning?

Reconceiving of the school as sacred space devoted to learning would allow us to make a number of conceptual shifts that are necessary to improve student learning in this country. We would first be able to distinguish between the kinds of activities that could occur in schools and those that should not. For example, if schools are indeed sacred space for learning, then should we be using them to sell wrapping paper?

The recommendations in the previous chapters are all premised on the belief that we must reconstruct our schools for learning. Put differently, they can be seen as ways of making the idea of sacredness concrete. I recommend doing away with the haphazard reenactment of schooling practices that have become mere rituals. If we view classrooms—the scenes of learning—as secular sacred spaces, we won't:

- allow bells to interrupt student engagement
- force teachers to waste important time taking attendance, etc.
- devote valuable school resources to placing a sports agenda above the interests of learning in the classroom
- use classrooms to raise money
- divert student attention away from learning with nonessential programs and agendas
- send important schoolwork home as homework

If we do view classrooms and classroom time as sacred, we will:

- create schedules that allow teachers to know their students well
- align the priorities of schools so they match our ambitions for students as learners
- clear the clutter out of schools by aligning the activity of the school day with the learning goals for our students

- shift the responsibility for extracurricular activities to the community
- provide a structure where all schoolwork can be completed under the guidance of a professional educator

I believe that talking about school as a sacred space is exactly the kind of "vision" that can generate specific and positive ideas for change in the here and now. Sacredness is a metaphor that suggests new ways of organizing the use of time and money in our public schools.

The idea of classrooms as sacred spaces is not indispensable to a vision for change; it is not a necessary aspect of my close analysis of how time and money get wasted in schools. If you buy my analysis but cringe at talk of "sacredness," that's fine with me. The arguments for change that emerge from analyzing how time and money are misspent stand on their own. Explicit, public standards for learning can be like lodestars in guiding the direction change should take. The real-world examples available of alternative ways to organize school provide more than enough inspiration and guidance for all school districts.

But for me the idea of school as sacred space provides a vocabulary that does justice to the importance we attach to education and gives us another layer of positive guidance. It sets the tone and framework for the conversation I believe we all should be having in our schools and homes and school board meetings and political campaigns about how to spend school time and money.

We claim to believe in the importance of education as a national goal. National commissions composed of the captains of industry meet to make declarations on the importance of education for our economy. Our self-image of American society as a learning society and of ourselves as number one in education, our rhetoric about life-long learning, all suggest the value and meaning that education has for us as a society. Our very identity as Americans is based on our notions of freedom and democracy, which we know can be sustained only if our citizens are well educated. Yet schools, the pubic institutions devoted to creating and sustaining our identity, are under-funded, underutilized, and overburdened. As I have said, they try to do too much and end up doing too little.

By suggesting that we see schools as sacred spaces dedicated to learning, I am suggesting what I hope will be a productive idea for shifting priorities away from wasted time and money, an idea that will inspire debate and practical proposals. The idea—like the book itself—is a tool. I hope people will find them useful as we together focus on spending school time and money in ways that reflect what we value most.

Notes

Introduction

1. Linda Darling-Hammond, *The Right to Learn: A Blueprint for Creating Schools That Work* (San Francisco: Jossey-Bass, 1997), p. 180.

1. The Fractured School Day

1. Sarah Huyvaert, *Time Is of the Essence: Learning in Schools* (Boston: Allyn & Bacon, 1998), p. 184.
2. Ibid.
3. National Center for Education Statistics. "Time in the Classroom," Indicator of the Month, publication no. ED 367 667 (Washington, D.C.: National Center for Education Statistics, 1998).
4. Ibid.
5. Fisher, cited in T. L. Good and J. E. Brody, *Looking in Classrooms* (New York: Harper & Row, 1987), p. 35.
6. David Berliner, "Tempus Educare," in P. L. Peterson and J. J. Walberg, eds., *Research on Teaching* (Berkeley, Calif.: McCuthan, 1979).
7. Ibid., 128.
8. B. Rosenshine, "How Time Is Spent in Elementary Classrooms." In C. Denham and A. Lieberman, eds., *Time to Learn: A Review of the Beginning Teacher Evaluation Study* (Washington, D.C.: National Institute of Education, 1980).

9. Good and Brody, *Looking in Classrooms.*

10. Ibid., p. 35.

11. Huyvaert, *Time Is of the Essence,* p. 34.

12. National Commission on Excellence in Education, *A Nation at Risk* (Washington D.C.: U.S. Government Printing Office, 1983).

13. Education Commission of the States, "Time for Results," *Education Week,* November 28, 1990.

14. J. A. Mazzarella, "Longer Day, Longer Year: Will They Make a Difference?" *Principal* 63, no. 5 (May 1984): 14–20.

15. C. E. Ballinger, N. K. Kirschenbaum, and R. P. Poimbeauf, *The Year-round School: Where Learning Never Stops* (Bloomington, Ind.: Phi Delta Kappa Educational Foundation, 1987).

16. Janie Funkhouser, Daniel Humphrey, Karen Panon, and Eric Rosenthal, *A Research Review: The Educational Uses of Time* (Washington D.C.: U.S. Department of Education, 1995).

17. National Education Commission on Time and Learning, *Prisoners Of Time* (Washington, D.C.: Office of Educational Research and Improvement, 1994), p. 2. The complete report is also available at www.ed.gov/pubs/PrisonersOfTime.

18. Ernest Boyer, *High School: A Report on Secondary Education in America* (New York: Harper Colophon Books, 1983), p. 232.

2. Who Could Be against Dental Health?

1. Larry Cuban, *How Teachers Taught: Constancy and Change in American Classrooms* (New York: Teachers College Press, 1993).

2. Julie Z. Aronson, "Stop the Clock: Ending the Tyranny of Time in Education," *Far West Laboratory,* February 1995, p. 8.

3. Cited in David Tyack, *The One Best System* (Cambridge: Harvard University Press, 1974), p. 231.

4. Herbert M. Kliebard, *The Struggle for the American Curriculum, 1893–1958* (Boston: Routledge, Kegan Paul, 1986), p. 125.

5. Lawrence J. Dennis, George S. Counts, and Charles A. Beard, *Collaborators for Change* (Albany: State University of New York Press, 1989).

6. Ibid., p. 118.

7. Lawrence Cremin, *American Education: The Metropolitan Experience, 1876–1980* (New York: Harper & Row, 1988), p. 309.

8. Dianne Ravitch, *Left Back: A Century of Failed School Reform* (New York: Simon & Schuster, 2000), p. 43.

9. Ibid., p. 49.

10. Cremin, *American Education,* p. 233.

11. Ibid.

12. Ravitch, *Left Back,* p. 124.
13. Linda Darling-Hammond, *The Right to Learn: A Blueprint for Creating Schools That Work* (San Francisco: Jossey-Bass, 1997), p. 182.
14. Marc Tucker and Judy Codding, *Standards for Our Schools* (San Francisco: Jossey-Bass, 1998), p. 75.
15. Ibid., p. 247.
16. Darling-Hammond, *Right to Learn,* p. 259.

3. Counting Costs

1. Ellwood P. Cubberley, *The History of Education* (Boston: Houghton Mifflin, 1920), p. 364.
2. U.S. Department of Commerce, Bureau of the Census, *Historical Statistics of the United States: Colonial Times to 1957* (Washington, D.C.: U.S. Government Printing Office, 1960), p. 207.
3. *Hazards Register of Pennsylvania* 15, no. 18 (May 2, 1835).
4. Michael W. Apple and James A. Beane, eds., *Democratic Schools* (Alexandria, Va.: Association for Supervision and Curriculum Development, 1995).
5. National Commission on Excellence in Education, *A Nation at Risk* (Washington D.C.: U.S. Government Printing Office, 1983). See also P. E. Drucker, *Post-Capitalist Society* (London: Butterworth-Heinemann, 1993); J. Avis, M. Bloomer, G. Esland, D. Gleeson, and P. Hodkinson, *Knowledge and Nationhood: Education, Politics, and Work* (London: Caswell, 1996).
6. Richard J. Murnane, "Interpreting the Evidence, 'Does Money Matter?'" *Harvard Journal on Legislation* 28, no. 2 (Summer 1991): 457.
7. Jonathan Kozol, *Savage Inequalities: Children in America's Schools* (New York: Crown, 1991).
8. Allan Odden, David Monk, Yasser Nakib, and Lawrence Picus, "The Story of the Education Dollar: No Academy Awards and No Fiscal Smoking Gun," available at Kappan on-line, www.pdkintl.org/kappan/kodd9510.htm.
9. Lawrence O. Picus and Minaz B. Fazal, "Why Do We Need to Know What Money Buys? Research on Resource Allocation Patterns in Elementary and Secondary Schools," in Lawrence O. Picus and James L. Wattenbarger, eds., *Where Does the Money Go? Resource Allocation in Elementary and Secondary Schools* (Thousand Oaks, Calif.: Corwin Press, 1995), p. 16.
10. Ibid., p. 18.
11. James Guthrie, "Implications for Policy: What Might Happen in American Education If It Were Known How Money Actually Is Spent?" in Picus and Wattenbarger, *Where Does the Money Go?,* p. 259.

4. The Sporting Life in Schools

1. Marc Tucker and Judy Codding, *Standards for Our Schools: How to Set Them, Measure Them and Reach Them* (San Francisco: Jossey-Bass, 1988).

2. The number of teacher-coaches varies depending on the size of the school, but what varies very little is that for each sport that a high school fields, at least two coaches are assigned. The problems associated with the teacher-coach are so numerous that many schools now have turned to "walk-on" coaches hired by the school just to coach a sport, especially for the "lesser" sports like golf and wrestling.

3. Tucker and Codding, *Standards for Our Schools,* p. 104; Lawrence A. Cronin, *American Education: The Colonial Experience, 1607–1783* (New York: Harper & Row, 1970); see also www.ed.gov/pubs/PrisonersOftime/Prisoners.html.

4. Jonathan Zimmerman, "Columbine and the Cult of High School Sports," *Philadelphia Inquirer,* May 22, 1999.

5. Robert Lynd and Helen Merrell Lynd, *Middletown: A Study in Modern American Culture* (New York: Harcourt Brace, 1929), p. 6.

6. Ibid., see chapters 13–16.

7. Ibid., p. 213.

8. Ibid., p. 212.

9. Ibid., *Middletown in Transition: A Study in Cultural Conflicts* (New York: Harcourt Brace, 1937), p. 291.

10. The Bapstonian, John Bapst High School Yearbook, Bangor, Maine, 2001.

11. H. G. Bissinger, *Friday Night Lights: A Town, a Team, a Dream* (Cambridge: Da Capo Press, 1990).

12. For an overview of the difficulties of calculating real costs in schools, see Lawrence O. Picus and James L. Wattenbarger, eds., *Where Does the Money Go? Resource Allocation in Elementary and Secondary Schools* (Thousand Oaks, Calif.: Corwin Press, 1995), p. 13. Harold Wheeler (former school board member, Union #98, Mt. Desert, Maine), private conversation, 2 June 2002.

13. Harold Wheeler, private conversation, June 2001.

14. Allan Odden, personal communication, October 10, 2001.

15. Eldon Snyder and Elmer Spreitzer, *Social Aspects of Sport* (New Jersey: Prentice-Hall, 1983), p. 105.

16. Tom Loveless, "How Well Are American Students Learning?," Brown Center Report on American Education (Washington, D.C.: Brookings Institution, 2001).

17. Thomas Toch, "Reformer Ross," U.S. News on line, June 1, 1992.

18. Kerry White, "Legislative Gamesmanship," *Education Week,* 1998.

19. L. S. Vygotsky, *Mind in Society* (Cambridge: Harvard University Press, 1978), p. 92.
20. See the web site of the International Association of a Child's Right to Play (www.ipaworld.org).

5. Zero-Based Budgeting

1. Carolyn D. Herrington, "The Politics of School-Level Finance Debate and State Policy Making," in Lawrence O. Picus and James L. Wattenbarger, eds., *Where Does the Money Go? Resource Allocation in Elementary and Secondary Schools* (Thousand Oaks, Calif.: Corwin Press, 1995), p. 248.
2. Ron Chilcote, "Prospects for Education in California," *Education Leadership* 36, no. 8 (May 1977): 570.
3. National Education Commission on Time and Learning, *Prisoners of Time* (Washington, D.C.: Office of Educational Research and Improvement, 1994).
4. Ron Chilcote, personal correspondence, September 10, 2001.
5. James Guthrie, "Implications for Policy: "What Might Happen in American Education If It Were Known How Money Is Spent?" in Picus and Wattenbarger, *Where Does the Money Go?*, p. 246.
6. Marge Scherer, "When the Day Is Over," Education Leadership 58, no. 7 (April 2001): 5.
7. Beth Miller, "The Promise of After School Programs," *Education Leadership* 58, no. 7 (April 2001): 7.

6. Restructuring Time, Restructuring Schools

1. Joseph Carroll, *The Copernican Plan: Restructuring the American High School* (Andover, Mass.: Regional Laboratory for Educational Improvement of the Northeast and Islands, 1989).
2. Laurie Olsen and Ann Jaramillo, "When Time Is on Our Side: Redesigning Schools to Meet the Needs of Immigrant Students," in *The Dimensions of Time* (Albany: State University of New York Press, 2000).
3. Deborah Meier, *The Power of Their Ideas* (Boston: Beacon Press, 1995).
4. For views of those in the standards-based reform movement, see especially Marc Tucker and Judy Codding, *Standards for Our Schools: How to Set Them, Measure Them and Reach Them* (San Francisco: Jossey-Bass, 1998), and Linda Darling-Hammond, *The Right to Learn: Blueprints for Creating Schools That Work* (San Francisco: Jossey-Bass, 1997); see also National Education Commission on Time and Learning, *Prisoners of Time* (Washington D.C.: U.S. Printing Office, 1994).
5. Etta Kralovec and John Buell, *The End of Homework: How Homework*

Disrupts Families, Overburdens Children, and Limits Learning (Boston: Beacon Press, 2000).

6. William Holland Drury, *Chance and Change: Ecology for Conservationists* (Berkeley: University of California Press, 1998), p. 202.

7. The Classroom as Sacred Space

1. Joseph P. McDonald, *Redesigning Schools: Lessons for the 21st Century* (San Francisco: Jossey-Bass, 1996).

2. Émile Durkheim, cited in Jonathan Smith, *Map Is Not Territory: Studies in the History of Religion* (New York: E. J. Brill, 1987), p. 90

3. Smith, *Map Is Not Territory,* pp. 88–146.

4. McDonald, *Redesigning Schools,* p. 62.

Suggested Readings

Finding your way through the labyrinth of books on schools and school reform is a daunting task even for those who are "school reform" junkies like me. The following list is intended to help an interested reader delve deeper into some of the ideas and suggestions discussed in this book. I included only books that I think can easily be used by communities that are ready to get serious about improving their schools. With one exception I have held myself to two books for each major idea discussed in *Schools That Do Too Much*. Some of the books provide background material that informed citizens need when participating in decision making about education. Others lay the groundwork for a rethinking of the way schools do business. Taken together, they represent some of the best and most innovative thinking about education today. A discerning reader will note that books on this list cover a wide range of ideological territory. Authentic school improvement will demand that we move beyond the contentious debate that passes for public discourse on education and consider many points of view.

Time and Learning

Gandara, Patricia, ed. *The Dimensions of Time and the Challenge of School Reform.* Albany: State University of New York Press, 2000. This collection of essays brings together the issues of time use in schools and school reform. A number of these essays are accounts of school-reform efforts that could provide blueprints for communities embarking on similar paths.

Huyvaert, Sarah H. *Time Is of the Essence: Learning in Schools.* Boston: Allyn & Bacon, 1998. Huyvaert shares the insights she gained from her work on the National Education Commission on Time and Learning.

Clarifying the Mission of Schools: Standards

Tucker, Marc S., and Judy B. Codding. *Standards for Our Schools: How to Set Them, Measure Them and Reach Them.* San Francisco: Jossey-Bass, 1998. The debate over standards is one of the most contentious in educational reform today. Most states have adopted statewide standards and schools are currently struggling to figure out how to help students reach them. In this collection, Tucker and Codding provide some insights in just how to use standards to the greatest advantage for children. In one compelling chapter, Codding tells the story of her attempts to override the culture of sports in the Pasadena High School, where she was principal.

Meier, Deborah, et al. *Will Standards Save Public Education?* Boston: Beacon Press, 2000. A lively collection of essays on the subject of standards, this book provides a foundation for understanding the range of issues in the standards debate.

Competitive Sports and Public Schools

Bissinger, H. G. *Friday Night Lights.* Cambridge: Da Capo Press, 1990. A moving account of high school football in the Texas town of Odessa. It may be easy to say, "Well, that's Texas, my town isn't like that," but the power of the book lies in the truth it uncovers about American values and educational priorities. A must-read for those interested in understanding the role of sports in the cultural life of American high schools.

Sperber, Murray. *Beer and Circus: How Big-time College Sports Is Crippling Undergraduate Education.* New York: Henry Holt, 2000. Understanding the role of competitive athletics in the high school is impossible without understanding the spectacle of big-time college sports.

Budgeting Issues

Picus, Lawrence O., and James L. Wattenbarger. *Where Does the Money Go? Resource Allocation in Elementary and Secondary Schools.* Thousand Oaks, Calif.: Corwin Press, 1995. This collection of essays, whose publication was sponsored by the American Education Finance Association, contains contributions worth wading through. They provide an informed reader with important background information about the issues that swirl around school budgeting. I remain amazed at the lack of information available to communities on school budgeting. I know of no book besides this one that lays out in clear and concise fashion the details of school budgeting or that provides guidelines for understanding the school budget.

School-Reform Recommendations

Linda Darling-Hammond. *The Right to Learn: A Blueprint for Creating Schools That Work.* San Francisco: Jossey-Bass, 1997. A comprehensive, readable blueprint for those committed to improving the schools in their communities, this book is suitable for use as the basis of community discussions and provides important examples against which educators can measure their school-reform initiatives.

Schorr, Lisbeth B. *Common Purpose: Strengthening Families and Neighborhoods to Rebuild America.* New York: Random House, 1997. One of the overarching themes of *Schools That Do Too Much* is that communities must be reinvented if we are to improve our schools. Schorr's chapter on schools is a refreshing examination of school reform from the perspective of a social analyst, providing great insight that professional educators often miss.

New Metaphors for Education

McDonald, Joseph P. *Redesigning School: Lessons for the 21st Century.* San Francisco: Jossey-Bass, 1996. McDonald challenges his readers to think deeply about schooling. By replacing our well-worn notions of school reform with some powerful new metaphors, McDonald's ideas can help communities rethink how they think about school reform.

Meier, Deborah. *The Power of Their Ideas.* Boston: Beacon Press, 1995. Meier's writing is so rooted in schools that we can practically hear the bells ringing as we turn the pages. In this work, Meier implores us take seriously the challenge of improving the educational experience of all American children and gives us the intellectual tools to do just that.

Finser, Torin M. *School Renewal: A Spiritual Journey for Change.* Herndon, Va.:
    Anthroposophic Press, 2001. Finser, who comes from the educational tradi-
    tion embodied in tbe Waldorf schools, shares his insights on ways to expand
    our understanding of community and how to achieve it in schools today.

Acknowledgments

I would like to thank the hundreds of parents and students who have asked me over the past two years, why can't kids get their school work done at school? Their questions helped me formulate the ideas that became this book. Students at College of the Atlantic have shared their educational lives with me, thus helping me to see more clearly some of the essential tensions in contemporary education. The suggestion that schools become sacred spaces is my solution to the crying need for schools to take the challenge of creating intellectually rigorous learning communities more seriously.

This book took surprising turns as current events overtook the smooth flow of writing: 9/11 came on the heels of my mother's death; both events affected me deeply and shattered much of what I had taken for granted. In relation to this book, I found I had written myself into positions that were opposed to what I had always believed to be the case about schooling. I heard the voices of my intellectual grandfathers as I questioned the role of schools in society, and I struggled as I found myself lining up with those who believe that standards are a way out of the educational morass that schools find themselves in. I would like to thank those at Beacon Press who struggled through these transitions with me, especially Helene Atwan and Andy Hrycyna. Marc Tucker, founder of the National Center for Education and the Economy, helped me understand the ways in which standards can be used to make educational opportunity more equitable, I would like to thank him for that insight.

I would like to thank the educators who questioned many of the ideas in this book, especially Barbara Neilly, principal of Emerson School; John Grasso, principal of Riverside School; and Susan Shields, reading specialist for the Los Angeles Unified School District. Their insights and careful reading and suggestions for this manuscript were most helpful. Their questions helped me more clearly articulate what I was trying to say.

I would especially like to thank my thoughtful research associate, Chelsea Mooser. Her careful attention to the ideas in this book and her skillful classroom observations have made this book richer. Bic Wheeler was a thoughtful and careful reader of the school stories in this book and assures me that the picture I paint of life in high school is, to quote Bic, "pretty much right." Many years ago, Ron Chilcote and I worked together trying to build a better budget for the Laguna Beach schools. I would like to thank him for supplying material from his files from that period. I would like to thank Charles Tetro, who gave me the freedom from work to complete this book and without whose support and encouragement this book would never have been possible.

Finally, I would like to thank my family and friends who were always willing to engage in a lively discussion about the ideas in this book and who were "critical coaches" for those ideas. Their insights, patience, and willingness to debate contributed to the overall structure of my arguments and suggestions for solutions.

Index